Bright Glory
Contents

BOOK 4

POETRY: Artists in Concert

BOOK 5

REALISM: Choices

BOOK 6

FANTASY: Hall of Mirrors

BOOK 7

SCIENCE: Animal Behavior and Communication

BOOK 8

NOVEL: The Pushcart War

BOOK 1

Maelstrom II

Think about the meanings of the words in the box below. Then choose a word to complete each of the following analogies.

euphoria	uncanny	incandescent
competent	predicament	

1. night : day :: misery : ___euphoria___

2. ___predicament___ : worrisome :: hurricane : windy

3. sympathetic : compassionate :: ___competent___ : able

4. ___uncanny___ : ordinary :: vague : specific

5. ___incandescent___ : glowing :: remote : distant

reprieve	appeal
paradox	incongruous

Write each of the words in the above box in front of its definition. Then write a sample sentence for each word.

6. ___paradox___ A group of facts, qualities, or circumstances that seem to contradict each other: _____

_____

7. ___appeal___ The transfer or request for transfer of a case from a lower court to a higher court for a new hearing: _____

_____

8. ___incongruous___ Not consistent with what is logical, customary, or expected: _____

_____

9. ___reprieve___ The postponement of a punishment: _____

_____

Maelstrom II

As Cliff faces death in his spacecraft, he recalls what happened to him, why it happened, and what he tried to do about it. Write each step Cliff took to try to solve his problems.

1. **Problem:** Cliff needed to find the least expensive return trip.
   Solution: He took the cheaper freight catapult instead of the shuttle.

2. **Problem:** Cliff knew something was wrong.
   Solution: Cliff called Launch Control.

3. **Problem:** Because the electric launcher broke down, the capsule never reached escape speed and would return in several hours to crash into the moon.
   Solution: The vernier rockets should boost the capsule into a moon-clearing orbit.

4. **Problem:** When the navigation rockets didn't work and Launch Control was silent, Cliff knew he was going to die.
   Solution: Thinking again about his present situation, Cliff bravely calls Myrna to tell her he's in trouble.

5. **Problem:** Cliff doesn't want to alarm his wife.
   Solution: He shows self-control in his talk to his family by thinking of them rather than himself.

6. **Problem:** Launch Control is still looking for a way to save Cliff.
   Solution: Cliff must jump from the capsule into space to change his orbit and escape the moon.

7. **Problem:** Cliff is haunted by a familiar feeling about the jump and can't pin down the memory.
   Solution: He recalls Poe's story about a fisherman who leaves his boat and ties himself to a barrel to escape a whirlpool, just as Cliff has left the capsule to escape his own maelstrom.

8. **Problem:** Cliff will run into the Soviet Range of mountains as he skims the moon's surface.
   Solution: The capsule, moving ahead of Cliff, blasts a gap in the mountains.

My First Death

Imagine that you are the copilot of an aircraft, and your job is to keep the daily log. As you complete the sentences below, use the words from the box that mean almost the same as the italicized words in the sentences.

colleagues	obligation	curiosity	catastrophe
unconscious	contrary	emotion	consciousness

Today was a *complete disaster* because we (Accept all reasonable answers that include the words shown in the answer space.) catastrophe

First, one of my *associates* became ill. All of my other colleagues

The person was totally *lacking awareness.* She must have unconscious

We were lucky because after only a few minutes she opened her eyes and *could understand what was happening.* But even though she had regained her state of consciousness

We all had *completely different* points of view about what to do next. Should we land and go to the doctor or continue the flight? It would be dangerous to land at this point. We all agreed that we should risk a landing except, of course, for the ill woman, who had a contrary

I felt we had a *sense of duty* to our friend, though. It was our obligation

Well, we never made it to a landing strip because a terrible storm blew in. We almost lost control of the aircraft. Our strong *feeling of fright* took over as we fought for our lives. This emotion

I used to have *a desire to know more* about aviation. I can now safely say that my curiosity

My First Death

Before Reading   Recall your predictions about "My First Death," and keep them in mind as you read the selection.

Read pages 44–48.   As you read, note events and ideas that are related by cause and effect. Then come back to this page and fill in the causes of the effects shown below.

After two to two and a half minutes, Guillaume would think Auriol was dead **because** a plane in a steep dive will crash within two to two and a half minutes.

Auriol was not saddened at the prospect of dying **because** she was too curious about what was going to happen to her when she died.

Auriol felt it was important to let ground control know what had gone wrong **because** usually the causes of crashes are a disturbing mystery.

Read pages 49–53.   As you read, pay attention to causes and effects. Then come back to this page and write the causes of the effects that are given.

Auriol thought that she probably had not heard Guillaume's communications while she was still in danger **because** her mind was too full of thoughts about what she was doing.

Auriol's friends on the ground had assumed that she was dead **because** she was not communicating with them and they could not see the plane.

The plane that Auriol was flying was difficult to control in a spin **because** it had swept-back wings instead of straight ones.

The plane could not be landed normally **because** it had been damaged by the stresses that it had undergone.

After Reading   Can you answer the *Thinking and Discussing* questions on page 54? If not, reread the selection, using the Stop and Think Strategy as needed.

My First Death

Write a word or phrase to complete each of the following statements.

1. Auriol plans to dive the plane and __make a sonic boom.__

2. Putting Auriol at risk, the plane goes from a controlled nose-dive into __a tailspin.__

3. Auriol thinks that the moment she is about to die is __the most interesting moment of her life.__

4. A surprised Auriol learns that she believes __that something will happen after death.__

5. Passing out and waking up again, she's determined to tell __ground control about the stabilizer failure.__

6. Although Auriol can't understand what Guillaume tells her, she remains __outwardly calm and continues to describe what is happening.__

7. Auriol remembers that to get out of a tailspin in a Mystère IV she should __speed up as much as possible.__

8. When Auriol pulls out of the nose-dive, she thinks __she will still hit the ground.__

9. Filled with __happiness at being alive__ , Auriol lands the battered plane.

10. Why, according to Auriol's account, is she able to pull the plane out of a spin and land a plane that is "all out of true"?
(Answers will vary.)

Of Men and Mountains

Use the context to help you define the italicized words in each group of sentences below. Then answer the questions that follow.

1. We carefully crossed over the *crevasse* on the *face* of the glacier. No one wanted to fall in.

   What is a *crevasse*? It is a deep crack or narrow gorge. _____

   _____

   What is a *face* as used in this context? A face is the front or the surface presented to view.

2. When you climb over the *crevice*, make sure not to lose your *purchase*. Be careful!

   What is a *purchase* as used in this context? A purchase is a grasp or a hold.

   What is a *crevice*? A crevice is a narrow crack or opening.

3. During our *ascent*, I strained the muscle in my leg. I can still feel *tension* in my leg when I stretch it out.

   What is an *ascent*? An ascent is an upward climb.

   How would you define *tension* as used in this context? Tension is a stretching or tightness.

4. The climb was a difficult *endeavor*, but we never lost our *composure*. I'm glad we made it to the top, but I don't have much energy left over in *reserve*.

   What is *reserve*? Reserve is something left over and available for use.

   _____

   What is an *endeavor*? Why might climbing a mountain be an endeavor? An endeavor is a major effort. It is often difficult to climb a mountain.

   _____

   Write a description of a mountain climber on a difficult endeavor. Use the vocabulary words in your description.

   _____
   _____
   _____
   _____
   _____

Of Men and Mountains

Before Reading   Recall your predictions about "Of Men and Mountains," and keep them in mind as you read the selection.

Read pages 58–63.   The first-person point of view used in this selection allows us to experience the narrator's thoughts and feelings. As you read, pay attention to how William O. Douglas feels, and imagine how his friend Doug might have expressed his feelings in the same situations. Then come back to this page and complete the chart.

(Sample answers)

Douglas's feelings:
His left hand feels paralyzed, his toes ache, his right arm is shaking, and he fears that he will cause Doug's death by not being able to hold him.

page 63
Doug can't find a toehold, and Douglas, who is supporting him, feels that he can't hold on much longer.

Feelings Doug might have expressed:
fear that he will fall, hope that Douglas's strength will hold out, determination to live

Read pages 64–67.   As you read the rest of the selection, note the feelings Douglas expresses and try to imagine being in Doug's place. Then come back to this page and complete the chart.

Douglas's feelings:
fear that he will not be able to hold on to the ledge, aching fingers and arms, sense of time stretching, fear, panic, fear that he is too weak to hang on

pages 66–67
Douglas hangs from his fingers after the ledge gives way beneath his feet.

Feelings Doug might have expressed:
fear for Douglas's life, determination to help Douglas

After Reading   Can you answer the *Thinking and Discussing* questions on page 69? If not, reread the selection, using the Stop and Think Strategy as needed.

Of Men and Mountains

The events in the box are out of order. Write them in the correct sequence on the lines that follow.

> Doug gives Douglas last messages for his family.
>
> After reaching the ground, they start up the northwest wall.
>
> Doug reaches a true cul-de-sac — he cannot go up and somehow must climb down.
>
> Standing on a 3-inch-wide ledge, Douglas holds and guides Doug's body 6 inches down to a toehold on the ledge below.

1. Douglas and his friend Doug try to climb the southeast front of Kloochman.

2. After climbing 600 feet, the boys reach a position where it looks like they can't go further.

3. Doug gives Douglas last messages for his family.

4. Doug jumps to the next ledge and pulls himself up by his arms.

5. Doug reaches a true cul-de-sac — he cannot go up and somehow must climb down.

6. Douglas hangs on to the rock about 12 feet from Doug's ledge.

7. Standing on a 3-inch-wide ledge, Douglas holds and guides Doug's body 6 inches down to a toehold on the ledge below.

8. After reaching the ground, they start up the northwest wall.

9. Douglas is 25 feet above Doug and 50 feet to his right when Douglas's ledge crumbles, leaving him hanging by his fingers.

10. Thinking of his father's last words, Douglas holds on until Doug rescues him.

11. Explain on the lines that follow why you agree or disagree with Doug that each of them had saved the other's life that day.

   (Answers will vary.)

Quicksand

The entry words and sample sentences are missing from these definitions. Complete each definition by writing the correct entry word and a sample sentence.

Entry Words

vise	livid	gaunt	probability	consolation
ford	insipid	taut	craving	circumstances

__taut__ — Pulled or drawn tight: **(Answers will vary.)** _____

_____

__livid__ — Deathly pale or white: _____

_____

__circumstances__ — Conditions or events connected with, and usually affecting, another: _____

_____

__ford__ — To cross by wading, riding, or driving through a shallow part of a stream or river: _____

_____

__probability__ — Likelihood that something will happen: _____

_____

__craving__ — A very strong desire: _____

_____

__vise__ — A metal tool, usually having a pair of jaws that open and close by means of a screw or lever: _____

_____

__gaunt__ — Thin and bony: _____

_____

__consolation__ — Comfort during a time of sorrow: _____

_____

__insipid__ — Lacking flavor; bland: _____

_____

Quicksand

Read the sentences below. Write "True" or "False." Then explain your answer on the line below.

(Sample answers)

1. Although near the Snake River, the children are sometimes thirsty. <u>True. They can't reach the water at times because of the high riverbank.</u>

2. John is hurt when everyone except Indepentia becomes scared of his strictness. <u>True. John notices when the children shrink from him.</u>

3. The Sager children's feet become more painful in the swampy river valley. <u>False. Their shoes remain pliable and comfortable in the swamp.</u>

4. John wades a river and realizes the bottom is quicksand. <u>True. The sand closes around his feet.</u>

5. By standing still every few moments, John crosses safely and very slowly. <u>False. He moves quickly and never stops moving his feet.</u>

6. When John tells Cathie to come along behind, he forgets to tell her not to stand still for a second. <u>True. He thinks the danger is obvious to all.</u>

7. Cathie hurries across without stopping but gets stuck in the quicksand anyway. <u>False. Cathie stops to catch a fish and gets stuck.</u>

8. John ties a rope around Cathie and ties the other end to his own waist. <u>False. John ties the rope to Walter the ox.</u>

9. Cathie is dragged out of the water, and the children build a fire to warm her. <u>True. The ox pulls her out.</u>

10. John decides they'll go on without resting. <u>False. John realizes they all must have a rest where they are.</u>

Dogsong

Complete the flow chart with the words from the box. Use the sentences to help you. Note that one word will be used twice.

headway	anticipated	recognized	diminished

1. If you planned for or foresaw an event, you − − − it.

2. When you make progress toward a goal, you are making − − −.

3. The word − − − means "got smaller or lessened."

4. The word − − − means about the opposite of *standstill* or *lack of progress*.

5. When you finally have seen something with which you are familiar, you have − − − it.

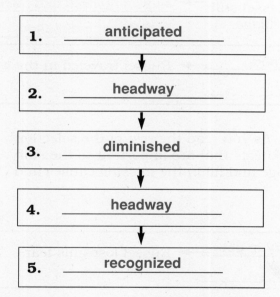

1. _____ anticipated

2. _____ headway

3. _____ diminished

4. _____ headway

5. _____ recognized

Use the flow chart as an outline to write a newspaper report about someone who was caught in a terrible storm. Make sure to use all the words from the chart.

_____

_____

_____

_____

_____

Dogsong

Before Reading   Recall your predictions about "Dogsong," and keep them in mind as you read the selection.

Read pages 92–97.   The plot and conflicts of the selection are developed mainly through a series of cause-effect relationships. As you read, look for cause-effect relationships. Then come back to this page and write the missing cause or effect for each pair below.

Cause	Effect
Oogruk wants oil and seal meat. →	**Russel goes seal hunting.**
A violent storm comes up suddenly. →	Russel takes shelter with his dogs.
The dogs don't want to run. →	**Russel forces them to run where he wants them to go.**
After traveling a long way, Russel still doesn't see the lights of the village. →	**Russel realizes that he has gone in the wrong direction.**
The ice plate Russel is on turned during the storm. →	Russel traveled in the wrong direction.

Read pages 98–102.   As you read the rest of the selection, look for other causes and effects that are important to the story. Then come back to this page and fill in the missing causes and effects below.

Russel makes a decision to try to get across the water. →	Russel loses his fear.
Russel pulls a chunk of ice across the water. →	**The chunk of ice forms a bridge.**
Russel throws the lead dog onto the ice bridge. →	**In a panic to get off the ice, the lead dog pulls the other dogs and the sled across to safety.**

After Reading   Can you answer the *Thinking and Discussing* questions on page 103? If not, reread the selection, using the Stop and Think Strategy as needed.

Dogsong

Write each step Russel takes to try to solve the following problems.

1. **Problem:** Oogruk wants lamp oil, seal meat, and seal fat.
   Solution: Russel takes the dogs out on the ice to harpoon a seal.

2. **Problem:** Russel uses up the daylight waiting out a storm.
   Solution: It's too dark to hunt, so he starts home.

3. **Problem:** The dogs don't want to go in Russel's direction.
   Solution: Russel forces the dogs to obey him.

4. **Problem:** Russel can't understand why he hasn't reached the village by this time.
   Solution: Russel figures out that the ice plate shifted during the storm.

5. **Problem:** Russel is worried and lonely, but the leader of the dogs seems to want to help.
   Solution: Russel decides to trust the dogs.

6. **Problem:** A narrow space of open water blocks the way home.
   Solution: Russel finds where the space has narrowed and hooks a floating ice chunk for a bridge.

7. **Problem:** The lead dog won't go on the bridge.
   Solution: When Russel throws him onto the ice chunk, he leads them all to safety.

Cause-Effect/Sequence of Events

Read the story below.

Canoeing from Camp Kimihakki

Lisa Franklin and Tess Rangley giggled as they carried an aluminum canoe onto the dock at Camp Kimihakki and slipped it into the slow, dark waters of the Saco River in southern Maine. Lisa threw a green knapsack and two oars into the midsection of the canoe and then, holding onto the edge of the dock with her left hand, stepped into the bow. Tess knelt down behind her in the stern of the canoe and grabbed a paddle.

"You ready for this?" Tess asked, barely suppressing another giggle. She had short, curly brown hair the color of maple syrup and sparkling brown eyes as dark as the waters of the Saco.

Lisa looked at Tess over her right shoulder and nodded. She hesitated a moment. Then her deep-set blue eyes regained their usual mischievous glow. "I'm ready if you are," she said.

Just then a loud bugle sounded reveille. "We'd better get going before somebody sees us," Tess said, a worried note catching in her voice. It was 6:30 A.M. Camp Kimihakki would soon be alive with campers and counselors dressing, showering, cleaning up the big tents, and eating oatmeal and buttered toast at the canteen. It might be an hour or two before the absence of Tess and Lisa would be noticed.

The canoe adventure was the result of a whispered pact Tess and Lisa had made the evening before as they sat around a campfire nibbling hot biscuits. The two teen-agers had agreed to wake up before dawn, borrow a canoe, and row off on a day-long adventure without telling another soul. Of course, the waterfront counselors would figure out what had happened as soon as they noticed the missing canoe. No one would be too worried — the girls had convinced themselves — because both were excellent swimmers and topnotch canoeists.

Now the sun peeked over the lush pine forest that sheltered Camp Kimihakki from harsh winds and penetrating light. Small clouds dotted the cornflower-blue sky. "We're off," shouted Lisa, leaning forward and plunging her long oak paddle into the smooth, shiny water. "E-e-e-y-a-a!!"

As they slipped downriver, the teen-agers laughed and chatted pleasantly. They paid scant notice to the passing scenery.

The two teen-agers traveled in this carefree fashion all day. Then, toward dusk, the canoe suddenly started bucking and dipping wildly. Without their noticing, Tess and Lisa had come upon some rapids. The canoe dove downward again. White sheets of water flew up on both sides. "Rapids!" Tess screamed. The front of the canoe struck a large rock and tipped over, dumping the girls into the water. They swam to shore, struggling in the strong current, and then knelt on the bank, gasping, exhausted. Lisa had managed to grab her waterproof knapsack; everything else, the canoe included, was gone. They were stranded.

Read the directions and answer the questions below.

(Sample answers)

1. Think of the four main events of the story so far in chronological order. Tell how one event leads to another.

   Tess and Lisa first make their pact, and then, in the morning, they take the canoe

   and paddle off. They float downriver and encounter some rapids. Their canoe

   overturns, and they swim to shore.

2. What cause-effect relationships are contained in the series of events?

   The trip is the result of a pact the girls have made; they do not notice the rapids

   because they are not paying attention; they are stranded because their canoe

   overturns.

3. What other cause-effect relationships can you find in the story?

   The girls think that the counselors will not worry *because* both are good swimmers.

   Tess is afraid they may be caught *because* reveille has sounded and the camp is

   coming to life.

4. How does knowing the sequence of events and their causes help build suspense?

   Knowing why events are happening helps the reader understand *what* is happening,

   and once the reader understands what is happening, the suspense builds because

   the events are plainly leading to an adventure of some kind.

   "Canoeing from Camp Kimihakki" continues on page 16.

Understanding Conflict and First-Person Point of View

The beginning of this story appeared on page 14. Finish reading the story about Lisa and Tess. Then answer the questions that follow.

Lisa pulled a worn brown book and a dull pencil out of her knapsack. Maybe if she sat down and wrote about her predicament, she'd get an idea. She glanced at Tess, curled up in a sunny spot of grass, finally asleep after a distressing night of chills and fever. Lisa read over the last entry in her diary, dated July 28, written two nights ago, right after she and Tess had decided to steal away from Camp Kimihakki for a joy ride on the Saco. Some joy ride, Lisa thought, as she began to write.

July 30

Dear Diary,

Here I am, somewhere on the Saco River, miserably lost, hungry, and scared. My friend Tess and I took off on Thursday morning for a canoe trip, just as we planned. We had a great time paddling, sunbathing, eating up the picnic lunch we stole from the canteen. We thought the whole thing was such a goof: two goody-goodies stealing food and a canoe for the day. Nobody would believe it! And now look at the spot we're in. I swear, I'll never even think about doing something this crazy again.

All the same, I'm trying to keep my sense of humor, trying to see the bright side of things. I don't want to lose my head or my hope. Somebody's going to find us, or we're going to find a way out of this. I just know it, and if I keep thinking this way, always positive like Dad and Mom taught us, I will get out.

Last night when Tess got sick, I told her all the jokes I could think of. I even got her to smile a couple of times, but I was worried. Her face was as white as this paper I'm writing on, and her eyes had lost their sparkle. I tried to get her to eat some of the blueberries I found, but she wouldn't. I hope it's just flu or a bad cold — not the result of being in the water when we fell in.

Now I'm not sure what to do next: let Tess rest here all day, wait for help, or try to take us back on foot. So far the weather's held out; it was warm even last night. But today it's cloudier than it's been all week.

What should I do? What's best for us both? As soon as Tess wakes up and I can tell how she's doing, I'll have to decide. Wish us luck.

Which part of the story is told from the first-person point of view? How can you tell?

Lisa's diary; she uses the first-person pronouns *I, my, we,* and *us.*

_____

In what ways does Lisa's first-person account have an effect on the reader?

The first-person point of view gives the reader insight into Lisa's thoughts and feelings. It also provides a sense of immediacy, allowing the reader to experience Lisa's conflicts right along with her.

_____

What are the conflicts that Lisa faces, and are they external (from without) or internal (from within)?

Lisa faces both internal and external conflicts. She has to fight against her own fear and loss of hope — those are internal conflicts. At the same time, she must fend for herself and Tess, who is ill, in the woods, with only the food she can forage and no certain way back to the camp — those are external conflicts.

_____

_____

_____

_____

On the basis of what you know about Lisa from her diary, what qualities does she seem to have that help her to face the conflicts?

She has a sense of humor and a positive outlook on life. She also appears to be strong, thoughtful, and intelligent.

_____

Do you think the first-person point of view is especially well suited to adventure stories? Why or why not? Explain.

(Answers will vary.)

_____

_____

_____

_____

_____

_____

_____

BOOK 2

The Ballad of John Henry

Read the sentences below. Use the context to help you determine which word from the box to write in the blank. Then write the meaning of the word. If you need help, use your Glossary.

steel	hammer	steam drill	shaker

1. Today there are all sorts of construction equipment, but years ago a _____**hammer**_____ and a nail were two of the best building tools people could find. **(Answers will vary.)** _____

_____

_____

2. An alloy of carbon and iron, _____**steel**_____ is one of the strongest, most durable substances that exist. It is no wonder that Superman was often compared to it. _____

_____

_____

3. It took great strength and endurance for the _____**shaker**_____ to hold the drill in place as the steel driver pounded the hammer again and again. _____

_____

_____

4. The _____**steam drill**_____ was a huge and noisy machine that drilled through heavy rock and steel. It was powered by a steam engine and was thought to be more powerful than a human. _____

_____

_____

Use the words in the box to complete the following analogies.

paintbrush : painter :: _____**hammer**_____ : carpenter

bulldozer : ditch :: _____**steam drill**_____ : tunnel

paper : book :: _____**steel**_____ : bridge

The Ballad of John Henry

Before Reading   Recall your prediction about "The Ballad of John Henry," and keep it in mind as you read the selection.

Read the selection.   Like most folk heroes in legends, John Henry has been exaggerated. As you read, look for ways in which he is made to seem larger than life. Then come back to this page and fill in the chart.

Exaggeration	What It Says About John Henry
Stanza 1: As a baby, he picks up a hammer and a piece of steel.	He is strong.
As a baby, he speaks.	He is unusually advanced.
He predicts the cause of his death.	He is superhuman.
Stanza 5: Using his hammer and steel, John Henry works faster than a steam drill.	He is powerful and determined.
Stanza 7: The captain says the mountain is sinking in from the blows of John Henry's hammer.	He is powerful.
Stanza 10: John Henry hammers until his hammer catches fire.	He is powerful, determined, and tireless.

After Reading   Can you answer the *Thinking and Discussing* questions on page 117? If not, reread the selection, using the Stop and Think Strategy as needed.

The Ballad of John Henry

Complete the story map below. Look back at the story if you need help.

(Sample answers)

Setting the mountain by the Big Bend Tunnel on the C&O Railroad

Main character John Henry

Minor character the captain

Plot

Beginning The baby John Henry, sitting on his mother's knee, says a hammer and steel will cause his death someday.

Middle When John Henry sees how little he is compared to the mountain, he breaks down and cries.
Then he says he'll die before he will give up.

Climax With his powerful arm, John Henry drills five feet deeper than the steam drill.

Conclusion John Henry hammers until the hammer catches fire and he dies.

What do you think accounts for the lasting popularity of this ballad?

(Answers will vary.)

_____

_____

_____

Tony Beaver

The word in the center of each word web appears in "Tony Beaver." Complete the webs by filling in the circles with the following words: *overwhelmed, protection, undertow, embankment, burdened, flooded, dangerous, safety, stream.* Add more circles for other words you associate with the center word.

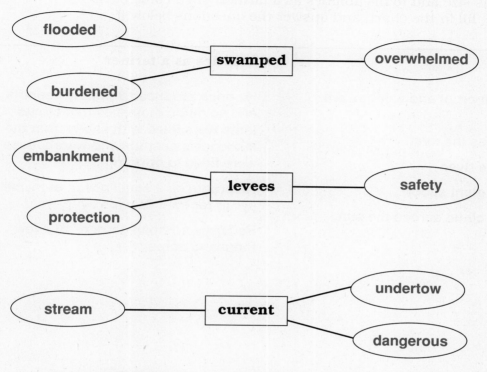

Use the words from each web to write a description of a river in a storm.

_____

_____

_____

_____

_____

_____

_____

_____

_____

_____

_____

Tony Beaver

Before Reading   Recall your prediction about "Tony Beaver," and keep it in mind as you read the selection.

Read the selection.   Tony Beaver is a bigger-than-life folk hero. As you read, look for exaggerated statements and events related to his size and to his abilities as a farmer. Then come back to this page, fill in the chart, and answer the questions below it.

Size	Abilities as a farmer
His vinegar cruet and salt box are huge.	He once produced so many peanuts and so much molasses that circus tents were filled with shells from the audience's peanuts and warehouses were filled to bursting.
He straddles the river.	
He stirs the river.	He produced a small ocean of maple syrup for Paul Bunyan every year.
He uses a giant spoon.	
He pulls a cloud across the sun.	He farms a "small garden" of a few thousand acres.

What action shows us that Tony is respected and looked up to by the townspeople? __The townspeople ask him if he can do something to stop the flood.__

_____

_____

What actions show that Tony is friendly? __He shakes hands with all the committee members who come to him for help, and he introduces children to the treat of peanut brittle.__

_____

After Reading   Can you answer the _Thinking and Discussing_ questions on page 125? If not, reread the selection, using the Stop and Think Strategy as needed.

Tony Beaver

Tony Beaver raises molasses maple trees, which produce oceans of delicious syrup every year, and he produces so many peanuts that he can't get rid of them all. Now a rainstorm threatens to wash away Eel River Landing.

Write Tony's solutions for these problems on the lines below.

1. **Problem:** Tony has too many peanuts and too much syrup.

   Solution: He has the townspeople throw the extra peanuts and syrup in the Eel River to stop the flooding.

2. **Problem:** To dam the Eel River and save the town, Tony must add enough salt and vinegar to the river to turn the syrup into candy.

   Solution: Oxen drag his vinegar cruet and salt box to the river.

3. **Problem:** Tony must cool the syrup so it will harden.

   Solution: He drags a cloud across the sun to stop the sunlight.

4. **Problem:** People need something to eat when they skate on the smooth brown lake.

   Solution: They eat the dam — Tony's invented peanut brittle.

Pecos Bill and His Bouncing Bride

Use the context of the following paragraphs to define the italicized words. Then use each word in a sentence.

Grandpa's favorites in any parade were the horses, all lined up in a magnificent *procession*. They reminded Grandpa of the Old West. He missed the days when he rode everywhere on horseback, before cars and pickup trucks became common.

"No siree, son," he said, "in my day, cars used to be quite a *novelty*. Nobody had them, and nobody saw them much, and when you did, more often than not, you were annoyed and *offended* by their noise and their smell. Yes sir, we thought cars were noisy and smelly *contraptions*, and we hoped they'd all disappear by morning. To this day, I believe there's nothing better than a horse.

"But most people *relented* and changed their minds when they saw how fast and far those cars could go. And you didn't have to feed them or give them water to drink, either."

My grandpa became *solemn* and stated seriously, "But a car will never replace a horse. Never. A car can't nuzzle your arm or sniff your pocket for sugar. A car can't love you like a critter."

procession: **(Answers will vary.)** _____

_____

_____

novelty: _____

_____

_____

offended: _____

_____

_____

contraptions: _____

_____

_____

relented: _____

_____

_____

solemn: _____

_____

_____

Pecos Bill and His Bouncing Bride

Before Reading   Recall your prediction about the conflict of "Pecos Bill and His Bouncing Bride," and keep it in mind as you read the selection.

Read the selection.   As you read, pay attention to the major events in the selection. Notice where they take place and which main characters are involved. When you have finished reading, fill in the main elements of the story below.

Summarizing the Story

Setting in Texas, on the prairies, at the I.X.L. Ranch, and at the Perpetual Motion Ranch

Main characters Pecos Bill, Widow-Maker, Slue-Foot Sue

Major problem Pecos Bill tells Slue-Foot Sue that he will grant her every wish, and she says that she wants to ride Widow-Maker. Bill, however, has promised the horse that no one else will ever sit in his saddle.

How the problem is resolved Sue jumps on Widow-Maker before Bill can stop her. She gets thrown, she bounces for a week, and when she stops she doesn't love Bill anymore.

Major events

1. Bill catches and breaks Widow-Maker.
2. Bill falls in love with Slue-Foot Sue.
3. On his wedding day, Bill promises Sue her every wish.
4. Sue jumps on Widow-Maker and starts bouncing.
5. Sue stops loving Bill.
6. Bill rides off and is never seen again.

After Reading   Can you answer the *Thinking and Discussing* questions on page 135? If not, reread the selection, using the Stop and Think Strategy as needed.

Pecos Bill and His Bouncing Bride

Complete each incomplete sentence in the paragraphs below. Look back at the selection if you need help.   (Sample answers)

Pecos Bill loves his horse Widow-Maker so much that he asks him to be his partner at the I.X.L. Ranch. He makes the horse two solemn promises. The promises are that __he will never use a bit,__ __and no other human will ride him__.

When Bill sells the Perpetual Motion Ranch to an English duke, he falls in love with __Slue-Foot Sue, the duke's daughter__. Bill learns fancy manners to please Sue's mother, the duchess, although __his friends make fun of him__. He asks Slue-Foot Sue __to marry him__.

Overcome by Sue's beauty, Bill makes her a solemn promise __to grant anything she wants__. Of course Sue __wishes to ride Widow-Maker__. Bucked off immediately, Sue lands on her bustle and __bounces for a week__. When she comes down at last, the wedding is off, and after a while, the unhappy cowboy __rides away on Widow-Maker__. None of the boys ever see him again.

Choose what appears to be the most exaggerated incident in this story and give reasons for your choice on the lines below.

(Answers will vary.) _____

_____

_____

Four Brothers Who Were Both Wise and Foolish

Each italicized word in the sentences below is a synonym for one of the words in the box. On the lines after each group of sentences, write the word from the box that has almost the same meaning as the italicized word. Then write an original sentence using the vocabulary word.

fancy	scoffed	serpent	simpleton

1. Now that I am fifteen, I have been granted a small fortune. For the first time in my life, I can afford to act on any *impulsive idea* that I have. I can buy whatever I *desire*. **fancy**

2. But there is one thing I must do to prove myself worthy of this fortune. I must find and slay an underwater *monster*, a terrifying *snakelike dragon*. **serpent**

3. Many of my fellow villagers *showed scorn* at my plans to defeat such an opponent. They *ridiculed* my strength and determination, not believing for a minute that I could succeed. **scoffed**

4. When I returned victorious to my village, I proved to the doubting villagers that I was no *numskull*. But sometimes I wonder if my fortune was really worth the battle. I am wise enough now to realize that a fortune alone cannot make me happy, and I was a *fool* to think it could. **simpleton**

Use the vocabulary words to complete these analogies.

1. discouraged : attempt :: _____**scoffed**_____ : idea
2. trunk : straight :: _____**serpent**_____ : coiled
3. pauper : millionaire :: _____**simpleton**_____ : genius
4. love : hate :: _____**fancy**_____ : reject

Four Brothers Who Were Both Wise and Foolish

Before Reading Recall your predictions about "Four Brothers Who Were Both Wise and Foolish," and keep them in mind as you read the selection.

Read pages 137–139. As you read, look for examples of irony — contrasts between what you would expect and what actually happens, or between what is said and what is meant. Then come back to this page and explain each example of irony given below.

Irony	Explanation
The father gives his four sons one peso, saying it is his fortune. He tells them to divide it and go into the world to follow their dreams.	A peso is next to nothing – hardly a fortune. It would buy very little, and certainly not one's dream.
The man with the glasses comments that he is looking at "not much," just China, and that the glasses are tiresome.	Being able to see all the way to China is incredible, and it seems that it would be marvelous, not tiresome, to have glasses through which you could see anywhere in the world.

Read pages 140–142, looking for more instances of irony. Then come back to this page and explain the examples of irony below.

The king has been too busy with important affairs of state to rescue his daughter.	You would expect that the princess would be more important to the king than affairs of state, and that rescuing her would have been his priority.
The princess wants to go to the farm with Bernardo, saying she has always wanted to milk a goat.	It's strange that a princess would want to do something as humble as milk a goat on a farm. Most story princesses want to marry princes and live in castles.

After Reading Can you answer the *Thinking and Discussing* questions on page 143? If not, reread the selection, using the Stop and Think Strategy as needed.

Four Brothers Who Were Both Wise and Foolish

Complete each incomplete sentence below. Look back at the selection if you need help.

(Sample answers)

1. A Spanish farmer's three oldest sons are _wild and reckless and want adventure_, but Bernardo, the numskull, loves to _stay at home and farm._

2. Giving his sons a silver peso to share, the farmer tells them _to go wherever they want to seek their fortunes._

3. Ricardo, Roberto, and Alfredo decide to _look for their fortunes separately and to meet again after a year._

   They persuade Bernardo, the numskull, who _wants to go home, to go west instead._

4. Ricardo ends up as a robber chief when _robbers take his quarter-piece_. Roberto becomes a great marksman when _he buys a gun_, and Alfredo buys _magic spectacles._

5. Bernardo pays to _become a coppersmith._

6. Together again, the four brothers attempt to _rescue a princess from a serpent._

7. Alfredo sees the princess, Ricardo steals her, and Roberto shoots the serpent. But when the serpent's tail almost splits the ship, Bernardo, the numskull, _mends the ship and saves the day._

8. The king says Bernardo will marry the princess because he rescued her, but because Bernardo would rather go home, _the princess accompanies him._

When Shlemiel Went to Warsaw

berate	dilemma	consultation	prankster

After reading each definition below, write on the line before it the correct vocabulary word from the box.

1. _____consultation_____ A conference in which advice is given or views are exchanged

2. _____berate_____ To scold severely

3. _____prankster_____ A person who plays mischievous tricks or jokes

4. _____dilemma_____ A situation that requires a person to choose between courses of action that are equally difficult or unpleasant

Now answer the following questions. Try to use the italicized words in your answers.

1. Is a *prankster* usually funny? Explain. (Answers will vary.) _____

_____

2. Would someone feel uncomfortable as he or she was being *berated*?
Why or why not? _____

_____

_____

3. Why might the saying "between a rock and a hard place" describe a
dilemma? _____

_____

_____

4. Describe a situation where a *consultation* might be important. _____

_____

_____

When Shlemiel Went to Warsaw

Before Reading Recall your prediction about "When Shlemiel Went to Warsaw," and keep it in mind as you read the selection.

Read pages 144–151. As you read, notice that numskulls show exaggerated foolishness in their silly and illogical reactions to events. Then come back to this page and explain the exaggerated foolishness about each of the situations below.

Shlemiel's method of setting out for Warsaw	Shlemiel sets off with no preparation, going down a street called Warsaw Street because he assumes it must go to Warsaw.
Shlemiel's response when he arrives back in Chelm	Instead of realizing that he has returned home, he assumes he has come to a second Chelm exactly like his hometown, and that everything and everyone he sees is a duplicate.

Read pages 152–156. Then come back to this page and explain the exaggerated foolishness of the characters' responses to the situations below.

How the Elders deal with Shlemiel's situation and his story	Because Shlemiel insists that he could not have turned around and returned to Chelm, the Elders accept his explanation that there is another Chelm. They agree that another Shlemiel will return.
The Elders' explanations for why Shlemiel never returned to Chelm	All their explanations involve impossible fantasies, such as cannibals, demon princesses, and a flat earth.

After Reading Can you answer the *Thinking and Discussing* questions on page 157? If not, reread the selection, using the Stop and Think Strategy as needed.

When Shlemiel Went to Warsaw

Write each plot element and event where it belongs in the diagram below. Look back at the selection if you need help. **(Sample answers)**

Event   The Elders decide Shlemiel must stay in the Chelm Two poorhouse until the real Shlemiel returns.

Event   Shlemiel's wife needs a Shlemiel to baby-sit so she feeds the crazy Shlemiel a good meal and makes up a fresh bed.

When the other Shlemiel never returns, Shlemiel doesn't know what to think but sees no point in traveling if it leads nowhere.

The Elders pay Shlemiel to live in his own house and help with the children until the real Shlemiel comes back.

Event   The townspeople ask the Elders what to do with Shlemiel.

When Shlemiel is turned around on his way to Warsaw, he believes he is in Chelm Two, not Chelm.

Write what you think changed for Shlemiel and what stayed the same. **(Answers will vary.)**

_____
_____
_____
_____
_____
_____

Problem

When Shlemiel is turned around on his way to Warsaw, he believes he is in Chelm Two, not Chelm.

Plot
Events: Rising Action

Event: Shlemiel's wife needs a Shlemiel to baby-sit so she feeds the crazy Shlemiel a good meal and makes up a fresh bed.

Event: The townspeople ask the Elders what to do with Shlemiel.

Event: The Elders decide Shlemiel must stay in the Chelm Two poorhouse until the real Shlemiel returns.

Climax

The Elders pay Shlemiel to live in his own house and help with the children until the real Shlemiel comes back.

Conclusion

When the other Shlemiel never returns, Shlemiel doesn't know what to think but sees no point in traveling if it leads nowhere.

Brother Coyote and Brother Cricket

Read the four newspaper articles about a debate between a lion and a mouse. Choose the word from the box that best describes each article. Then use the word in a headline for the article. Write each headline above each article.

terms	vanity	summoning	shrewder

(Sample answer) Debaters Name Their Terms

Yesterday Lion and Mouse had a disagreement about their territories. Mouse challenged Lion to a debate. At first, Lion laughed at the thought. But after much discussion, he and Mouse finally agreed on the necessary requirements and conditions for their debate.

(Sample answer) Mouse Summons Courage by Summoning Friends

As the date of the debate approaches, Mouse admits to being nervous. He feels that if his friends are near him, he will be able to benefit from their support. He has begun to send for all his friends, requesting that they appear at the debate and give him their encouragement.

(Sample answer) Lion Shows His Vanity

Lion, unlike Mouse, is feeling quite confident about the debate. After all, he is king of the forest. He lets everyone know that he doesn't need help, and never even considers apologizing for his excessive pride.

(Sample answer) Mouse Proves Shrewder

When the debate began, Mouse entered the room to a multitude of cheering friends. Lion was met with silence and an occasional hiss. King of the forest he may be, but it was obvious that his heart sank, and his confidence wavered. It seems that Mouse's approach was the more clever and practical indeed.

Now write your own article about a conflict between two animals. Try to use the vocabulary words in your article.

_____

_____

_____

_____

Brother Coyote and Brother Cricket

Before Reading   Recall your prediction about "Brother Coyote and Brother Cricket," and keep it in mind as you read the selection.

Read pages 159–160.   As you read, notice how Brother Coyote uses sarcasm — seemingly harmless remarks that are actually insulting. Then write the real meaning of each sarcastic remark referred to below.

(Sample answers)

Sarcastic Remark	Meaning
Coyote says that maybe Cricket will fill the hollow in one molar.	**You are small and practically worthless.**
In talking about fighting Cricket, Coyote says that maybe "the people need a comedy."	**Fighting against an enemy as small and harmless as you will be comical.**
Coyote says that he is trembling at the sight of Cricket's armor and weapons.	**There is obviously nothing about you that can harm me.**
Coyote addresses Brother Cricket as "General Cricket."	**Your talk of armies and of a serious fight between us is ridiculous.**

Read pages 161–162.   As you read, look for examples of exaggeration. Then answer the question below.

How does the writer use exaggeration in describing how Brother Coyote and Brother Cricket gather their armies?
He talks of Coyote's going east, west, north, and south, calling for *all* the creatures with claws and teeth. Likewise, Cricket gathers all the creatures in the area that have stingers and can stick.

After Reading   Can you answer the *Thinking and Discussing* questions on page 163? If not, reread the selection, using the Stop and Think Strategy as needed.

Brother Coyote and Brother Cricket

Read each false statement below. Then write why it is false.
(Sample answers)

1. A coyote likes to eat a fat cricket more than watermelon. **The coyote likes watermelon better.**

2. Brother Cricket asks only that Brother Coyote wait until the next day before eating him. **Brother Cricket says the coyote hasn't given him a chance.**

3. Brother Coyote suggests a duel with Brother Cricket. **Brother Cricket suggests the duel.**

4. Brother Coyote is terrified by the thought of Brother Cricket's army. **Brother Coyote is laughing at the thought.**

5. The next day, the fox reports that he can see no sign of General Cricket's army. **General Coyote, not the fox, can't see the army.**

6. At high noon, General Coyote attacks with all his forces. **Before noon, stung by hornets, General Coyote's army retreats.**

7. General Coyote learns that General Cricket is not as smart as he is. **General Coyote learns that he isn't as smart as the cricket.**

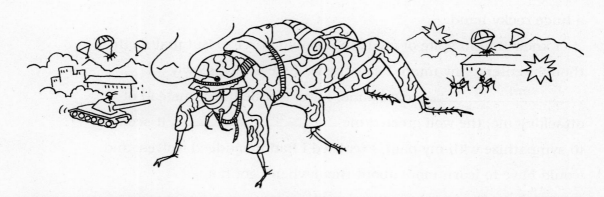

Coyote and Little Blue Fox

Think about the meanings of the words in the box. Then complete the paragraphs by writing the correct words on the lines.

agony	ambling	arduous	enmity
genially	retrieve	thwarted	tortuous

Some people say that these mountains are the most rugged in the land. I must climb to the top to escape the wolf that is on my trail. My legs and feet ache. Each step up the winding, twisting, __tortuous__ path is painful. But I am determined to continue. Although it is difficult and demands great effort, I will finish the __arduous__ journey.

As the sun began to set, I was distracted for a moment by its beauty and lost my footing. My walking stick tumbled down and caught between two boulders. I had passed the tree line and knew there would be no chance of replacing the stick. I bravely inched down the steep rock to where the stick was lodged. I balanced myself precariously and reached down to __retrieve__ it. But as I did so, I lost my grip on the rock and tumbled down the mountain. Bruised and battered, I cried out in __agony__.

I landed on a grassy shelf of the mountainside. I tried to lift myself up, but each attempt was __thwarted__ by a sharp pain in my right arm. I was so angry and frightened that I suddenly felt a great __enmity__ toward the mountain. I forced myself to be thankful that the mountain had also broken my fall like a huge rocky hand.

I knew that in spite of my pain, I would survive. But just as this thought entered my mind, I saw the wolf stealthily, slowly __ambling__ toward me. I was terrified. But instead of attacking me, the wolf greeted me __genially__. It seemed to sympathize with my pain. I realized I had misjudged wolves, and would have to learn more about them when I got home.

Coyote and Little Blue Fox

Before Reading Recall your prediction about "Coyote and Little Blue Fox," and keep it in mind as you read the selection.

Read pages 164–166. Like other characters in traditional tales, Coyote and Little Blue Fox have certain set characteristics that define their personalities. These character traits are established largely through exaggeration. As you read, look for events that exaggerate the traits in the boxes below. Then come back to this page and note those events in the boxes.

(Sample answers)

Coyote is conceited.

He takes Fox's suggestion to hide in the tree as his own.

He takes Fox's suggestion to tie a stone around his neck as his own idea.

He says that he is strong enough to hold up the cliff alone.

Coyote will believe anything.

He believes that Fox will share the prairie chickens with him and then allow himself to be eaten.

He believes the cliff is falling and that Fox will return with a log. He pushes against the cliff all day.

He believes that the moon's reflection is a maize cake.

He keeps believing Fox, no matter how many times he is duped.

Little Blue Fox is clever.

He dreams up the story of the prairie chickens and gets Coyote to climb the pine tree.

He thinks of the falling cliff story and gets Coyote to believe it and to hold up the cliff while he escapes.

He thinks up the story of the maize cake and persuades Coyote, with a stone around his neck, to jump in after the cake.

Little Blue Fox is calm and fearless.

He shows no fear but instead responds to Coyote's threats with clever ideas.

He waits for Coyote at the cliff.

He waits for Coyote at the lake.

Read pages 167–172. Then write in the boxes the rest of the events that exaggerate the character traits of Coyote and Fox.

After Reading Can you answer the *Thinking and Discussing* questions on page 173? If not, reread the selection, using the Stop and Think Strategy as needed.

Coyote and Little Blue Fox

The authors use words such as the ones listed below to create pictures of Little Blue Fox and Coyote. Decide which words suit each character and write them in the boxes.

gleefully   raging   thirsty   helpfully
chuckling   proudly   hasty   humiliated
hungry   thoughtfully   airily   laughing

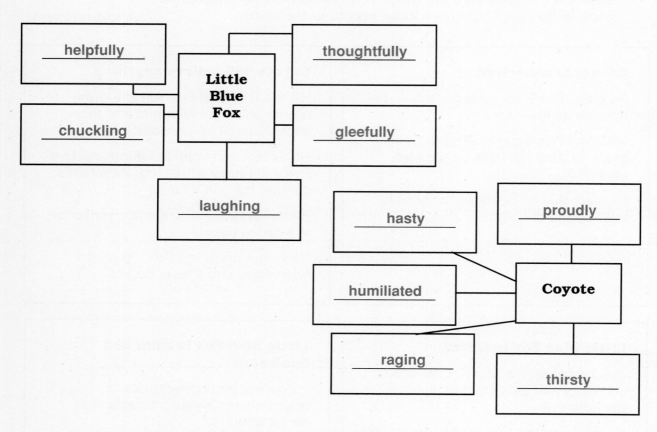

After each trick, write why you think Little Blue Fox was able to trick Coyote.

The prairie chicken trick   Coyote climbs the fir tree because <u>Coyote is greedy.</u>

_____

The cliff wall trick   Coyote holds up the wall because <u>Coyote is a showoff.</u>

_____

The maize cake trick   Coyote jumps in the lake with a stone around his neck because <u>Coyote is too hungry to stop and think.</u>

_____

The Story of the King's Lettuce

Match each of the words in the first column with its antonym from the second column by writing the correct letter in the blank.

1. __E__ complexities   **A.** unlikely
2. __A__ probable   **B.** attackers
3. __D__ perplexity   **C.** scanty
4. __B__ sentries   **D.** clarity
5. __F__ plausible   **E.** simplicities
6. __C__ sufficient   **F.** unbelievable

Write the correct vocabulary word on the line next to its definition. Then use that word in a sentence.

1. __sentries__ Persons, especially soldiers, posted at a

spot to warn of attackers or to check persons seeking admittance: _____

_____

_____

2. __complexities__ Things that are difficult to understand: _____

_____

_____

3. __plausible__ Appearing to be true or reasonable: _____

_____

_____

4. __sufficient__ As much as is needed; enough: _____

_____

_____

5. __probable__ Likely to happen or to be true: _____

_____

_____

6. __perplexity__ The condition of being confused or puzzled;

bewilderment: _____

_____

_____

The Story of the King's Lettuce

Before Reading   Recall your prediction about "The Story of the King's Lettuce," and keep it in mind as you read the selection.

Read pages 175–177.   As you read, look for exaggerated details of description. Then come back to this page and note those exaggerated details in the boxes below.

(Sample answers)

Kelfazin

It is the dreariest place in the world: There is no food but coarse grass, and the ground is too wet for digging.

King Darzin's kingdom

It is the biggest and richest animal city in the world.

The soldiers are very fierce.

The lettuce garden is guarded by a thousand sentries day and night.

Prince Rainbow

He has the power of the sky and the power of the hills, and Frith has given him the power to order the world as he thinks best.

The King's protection of the lettuce against El-ahrairah

He doubles the guard, and each gardener and weeder is checked by three guards.

Read pages 178–182.   Then write the exaggerated details of description in the appropriate boxes below.

Rabscuttle's reaction to eating the "diseased" lettuce

He moans and thrashes about, kicks in convulsions, rolls his eyes, gnaws at the floor, and foams at the mouth.

The promise Prince Rainbow keeps to El-ahrairah

He lets the rabbits out of the marshes, they multiply everywhere, and no power on earth can keep a rabbit out of a vegetable garden.

After Reading   Can you answer the *Thinking and Discussing* questions on page 183? If not, reread the selection, using the Stop and Think Strategy as needed.

The Story of the King's Lettuce

Write in the missing cause or effect for each item below.   (Sample answers)

1. **Cause:** Trapped with his people in the dreary marshes of Kelfazin, El-ahrairah feels responsible for their well-being.

   Effect: As a trickster hero, El-ahrairah makes a deal with Prince Rainbow to let his people leave the marshes of Kelfazin if he can steal the lettuces from King Darzin's garden.

2. **Cause:** Yona the hedgehog hears Prince Rainbow and El-ahrairah, and warns King Darzin.

   Effect: King Darzin doubles the guards on the lettuces.

3. **Cause:** Rabscuttle, El-ahrairah's Captain of Owsla, hides in the royal children's garden and makes friends with the prince.

   Effect: As the prince's friend, Rabscuttle safely enters the palace.

4. **Cause:** Rabscuttle goes to the storeroom and ruins all the food, including the lettuces.

   Effect: No matter what they eat, the king and all his people are sick for five days.

5. **Cause:** El-ahrairah cleverly disguises himself as a doctor and in a lofty manner demands to see the king.

   Effect: The guard is impressed by El-ahrairah's disguise and manner and takes him to the king.

6. **Cause:** El-ahrairah feeds Rabscuttle a lettuce to prove to the king that the lettuces really are infected.

   Effect: Rabscuttle's pretended convulsions convince the king that the lettuces will have to be thrown out.

7. **Cause:** Knowing the king's hatred of rabbits, El-ahrairah mentions that the infection is probably especially deadly to rabbits.

   Effect: Thinking he's very clever, the king has a thousand lettuces carried to the marshes to poison the rabbits.

8. **Cause:** Prince Rainbow sees the thousand lettuces piled at the marsh.

   Effect: Prince Rainbow keeps his part of the bargain and lets El-ahrairah's people out of the marsh, never to be kept out of a vegetable garden again.

Understanding Exaggeration

Read the following selection. Then answer the questions.

Tim Dimwhitten's Silver Lining

Tim Dimwhitten lived in a tiny, run-down shack on the edge of a small gray town called Treadmillen. His only companions were a lazy, flea-bitten dog and a sleepy, sad-sack donkey that hadn't moved for years.

Tim worked at a greasy little doughnut shop called Duke's Donuts. He spent his days cutting holes into circles of dough. Like his two companions, Tim was lazy and slow. He was so lazy and slow, in fact, that most of Duke's doughnuts didn't have holes. Tim didn't understand concepts like "ambition" or "hard work." Nevertheless, he dreamed of great riches: fabulous castles, beautiful princesses, sparkling jewels, and treasure chests full of gold.

Duke Donuts, Tim's master, was always complaining about Tim: "You're lazy, Tim," Duke would shout with irritation. "I've never seen a doughnut holer so slow. Wise up and learn the meaning of an honest day's work." But Tim went on holing doughnuts just as slowly as always.

One day a rich man came into Duke's Donuts and ordered a thousand glazed doughnuts. Tim studied the rich man with his fine jewels and his fancy pants. "Who's that?" Tim asked, after the rich man left with more doughnuts than Tim had ever holed in a month.

"Ach! That's Mr. Fancy Pants." Duke told him. "He's nothing but a robber — everything he owns he has stolen from poor widows and orphans."

"Aha," thought Tim. He had suddenly had an idea, the first, in fact, of his entire life. He was certain that the idea was a fine one indeed.

"I will become a robber like Mr. Fancy Pants," Tim said to himself, "and steal from widows and orphans, too. That's how I'll make my fortune."

That night, Tim waited behind a big oak tree near the main road just outside Treadmillen. He carried a club and a sack. With the club, he would scare the travelers he intended to rob. The sack he would fill with their riches. After a short while, a young woman in a forest-green hood came by on a pony. Tim jumped in front of the pony, grabbed its reins, shook his club at the young woman, and shouted, "Are you a widow?"

The woman looked puzzled. Tim shook his club again. Now the woman was terrified, for Tim was a big lunk. "N-n-no," she said timidly.

"Then be gone," Tim shouted with annoyance, and he let the woman and her pony pass.

1. List as many examples as you can find of the exaggerated character of Tim Dimwhitten.

(Sample answers)

Tim's only companions are a dog and a donkey — no people. Tim is so lazy and slow that most of his doughnuts do not have holes. Tim dreams of impossible riches. He has never had an idea in his life before coming up with his robbery scheme. His thinking is so literal that he doesn't consider stealing from the young woman simply because she isn't a widow.

2. What does the exaggeration contribute to the story?

The exaggeration reinforces the humor and creates a strong image of this particular numskull.

3. How does the exaggeration help identify a stock character in a traditional tale?

The exaggeration, together with the humor it creates, lets the reader know beyond a doubt that Tim is a numskull — a character meant to be laughed at.

4. What are some other examples of exaggerated ideas in the tale? How do they affect the tale?

The donkey has not moved for years. This is a funny idea in itself, and it reflects on Tim's character, because the two are companions. The rich man buys a thousand doughnuts. The effect is to reinforce the humor (a thousand doughnuts to go!) and to underscore the idea that Tim is lazy and slow, because he has never holed that many doughnuts in a month.

"Tim Dimwhitten's Silver Lining" continues on page 44.

Irony and Dialogue

The beginning of this story appears on page 42. Continue reading the tale of Tim Dimwhitten. Then answer the questions.

Next, a very old woman wrapped in a shawl walked past the oak where Tim Dimwhitten was hiding. Tim jumped out, blocking her path. Again he waved his club and shouted, "Are you a widow?"

Now, the old woman had seen many odd sights in her day, so she was neither surprised nor frightened by Tim's question. "I should say not, young man," she said. "I've been married sixty years, and I am on my way home to my husband."

"Then be gone," Tim shouted with even greater irritation than before.

The old woman moved on.

A few minutes later, a little boy came along the road with his puppy. When Tim leaped in front of him, the boy was scared. But then he saw Tim's face under the bright starlight. He knew right away — as he had been to Duke's Donuts before, and seen Tim loafing — that the big oaf in front of him was Tim Dimwhitten. So the boy knew that there was nothing to fear if he kept his own wits about him.

"Are you an orphan?" Tim asked the boy.

"Aye, that I am," the boy answered truthfully.

"Then give me your money or your life," Tim said.

The boy had sold a cow in Treadmillen just that afternoon. He was carrying the proceeds from the sale back to his orphanage. But the boy wasn't worried. He quickly thought up a plan. "I would gladly give you this tiny purse of silver," the boy said. "But I am in a hurry. I have no time to go back to the lake full of silver."

"What lake full of silver?" Tim asked.

"The lake where I filled this purse," the boy said. "Just look." The boy opened his purse, and, sure enough, it was full of silver, and it was soaking wet.

Tim grinned in triumph. He didn't stop to think that the boy might have dropped his purse in a puddle — which is exactly what the boy had done. Tim said, "Show me the way to the lake full of silver, and I will let you go free with your purse."

Soon Tim was trotting through the forest toward the lake. When he reached it, he grinned even more. The lake was full of silver — or so it seemed. Actually, the sparkling silver was only starlight glistening on the water.

Tim took out his sack and began to drag it through the lake. The water ran through the sack as if through a sieve. No silver! Tim tried harder and harder, and the harder he worked the wetter he got. Still no silver! Finally, the sun rose and the stars faded from the sky, along with their reflections in the lake. Tim was tired, and soaked to the skin. It was 6:00 A.M., time to get ready for another eight hours at Duke's Donuts, and Tim was as poor as ever.

Tim set out for the doughnut shop with a heavy heart. Had he not been so foolish, he might have realized that he had finally learned the meaning of an honest day's — or night's — work. But the lesson was as lost on him as the silver that had never existed.

1. In traditional tales, irony helps convey humor. How might you define irony?

   (Sample answers)

   Irony is the contrast between what is expected and what actually happens.

2. How might dialogue be used to create irony in a traditional tale?

   A stock character, such as a numskull, might say things people in real life would
   not say — or expect to hear said — if they were in the same situation.

3. What things does Tim Dimwhitten say that reveal him as a numskull?

   He asks the old woman if she is a widow, and tells her to "be gone" when she is
   not; he stupidly thinks he can rob only widows and orphans. Tim accepts the idea
   of the lake full of silver — something most people would dismiss as hogwash —
   and discusses it seriously with the boy.

4. What other examples of irony do you find in the tale?

   (Answers will vary.)

BOOK 3

Across the Centuries

Use the words in the box to complete the crossword puzzle.

aristocrat	occupation	disrupted	steppe
efficient	mandate	currency	money economy
prosperity	khan	dynasty	

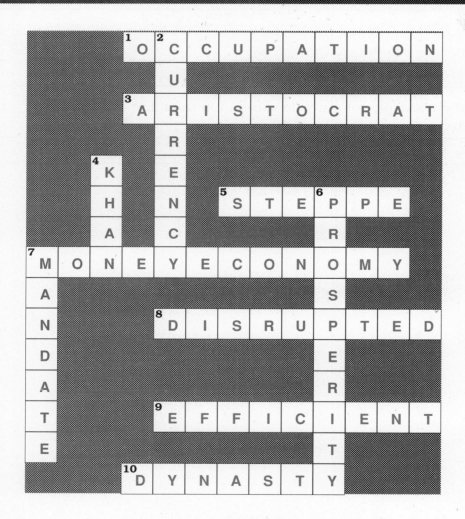

Across

1. The conquest and control of a nation or territory by a foreign military force

Down

2. Any form of money in actual use in a country

Across (continued)

3. A member of a social class based on inherited wealth, status, or sometimes title
5. A vast, somewhat arid plain
7. A system in which goods and services are purchased with coins and bills rather than in a direct exchange of goods and services
8. Interrupted or blocked the progress or functioning of
9. Acting or producing effectively with a minimum of waste, expense, and effort
10. A succession of rulers from the same family or line

Down (continued)

4. The titles of rulers of Mongol, Tatar, or Turkish tribes
6. The condition of being vigorous and healthy; success
7. An official command or instruction

Read the three newspaper articles below. Choose the word from the box that best describes each article. Then use the word in a headline for the article. Write each headline above each article.

prosperity	steppe	currency

(Sample answer) **Successful Effort to Save Steppe**

Seven years ago this week, a small group of concerned citizens met to consider ways to prevent destruction of the vast plain in this and surrounding counties. Efforts were being made at that time to convert the arid area into a heavily inhabited area. Plans included tearing up huge amounts of land. Yesterday, a spokesperson for the group met with reporters at Town Hall to announce that concerned citizens have succeeded in their efforts to save the environment.

(Sample answer) **Currency Change Confusing**

Residents of the country are having difficulty adjusting to a new set of coins and bills. When a customer goes to a cash register to make a purchase now, the amount looks completely different than it did only a week ago. Many people are using calculators to convert the new money figure into one that still makes sense to them.

(Sample answer) **New Money Encourages Prosperity**

Officials have issued a statement that lists the advantages of recent changes in the economy. First among these advantages is the promise of increased vigor and health. Citizens are guaranteed more success than the old systems could provide.

Across the Centuries

Complete each incomplete sentence below. Look back at the selection if you need help.

The Flowering of Chinese Civilization   (Sample answers)

1. From 617 to 1279, the Tang and Sung dynasties — rulers of China — encouraged <u>the works of artists, both poets and painters.</u>

2. During the Tang and Sung dynasties, people were chosen to work for the government civil service because <u>of their abilities.</u>

3. The Tang and Sung dynasties <u>built and improved roads and waterways</u> to connect different areas of China.

4. China became wealthy through <u>improvements in agriculture and the growth of</u> <u>trade.</u>

5. During this period, the Chinese invented <u>paper money, printing, gunpowder, and</u> <u>the compass.</u>

China and the Larger World

6. China was protected by <u>mountains to the southwest and desert to the west,</u> but the Mongols attacked <u>from the north across a grassy plain.</u>

7. In 1279, Kublai was the first Mongol leader to <u>rule all of China.</u>

8. The Yuan dynasty ruined much of China's farmland and gave <u>the important</u> <u>government jobs to other Mongols.</u>

9. The Yuan dynasty encouraged China's contact with the West by <u>sending camel</u> <u>caravans to the Black Sea and setting up postal stations across Asia.</u>

10. The first Ming emperor, Taitsu, defeated the Mongols in 1368 and

began the restoration of the empire when he resettled homeless

people, started public works projects, **seized large estates, raised the taxes of**
the rich, and abolished slavery.

_____

11. When the Ming emperors tried to prevent Chinese contact with the

West, traders and missionaries **carried information and inventions between**
China and the outside world.

_____

The First Emperor

Complete the analogies, using the words in the box below.

efficiency	excavation	archaeological	rebellious

geographical : maps :: ___archaeological___ : pottery

speed : bicycle racer :: ___efficiency___ : secretary

expedition : explorer :: ___excavation___ : archaeologist

adventurous : Christopher Columbus :: ___rebellious___ : Patrick Henry

In each group of words below, draw a line through the word that does not belong in the group, and then briefly tell how the other three words belong together.

rivals   opponents   competitors   ~~teammates~~

All words except *teammates* describe people who compete against each other.

ferocious   extreme   ~~content~~   intense

All words except *content* describe something very great or severe.

consolidate   ~~weaken~~   secure   strengthen

All words except *weaken* mean to make strong or firm.

unparalleled   unique   ~~common~~   unequaled

All words except *common* identify something that is special or one of a kind.

penetrate   puncture   pierce   ~~tear~~

All words except *tear* mean to pass into or through.

principles   ~~privacy~~   rules   ideals

All words except *privacy* refer to standards of behavior or beliefs.

The First Emperor

Before Reading Recall what you expected to learn from "The First Emperor," and keep those things in mind as you read the selection.

Read "The Tomb of the First Emperor" on pages 212–217.
As you read, pay attention to Ch'in Shih Huang Ti's place in history and the discovery of his fabulous tomb. Then come back to this page and write notes about the subjects below.

(Sample answers)

Ch'in Shih Huang Ti's accomplishments	Discovery and contents of Shih Huang Ti's tomb
founder of China, unified rival states, became emperor, built Great Wall of China, the name *China* comes from *Ch'in*	in 1974 peasant uncovered life-sized clay statue of warrior; spirit army of 6000 statues; 3-acre underground chamber

Read "Advice to the First Emperor" on pages 218 and 219.
Then summarize the advice of each sage below.

Hanfeizi's advice	Li Si's advice
The wise ruler uses methods that will keep the majority of his people from doing evil.	An intelligent ruler applies severe punishments to prevent rebellion.

After Reading   Can you answer the *Thinking and Discussing* questions on page 220? If not, reread the selections, using the Stop and Think Strategy as needed.

The First Emperor

Complete each incomplete sentence below. Look back at the selection if you need help.

(Sample answers)

The Tomb of the First Emperor

1. Ch'in Shih Huang Ti was important in Chinese history because <u>he founded</u> <u>China.</u>

2. When Ch'in Shih Huang Ti had conquered his rivals, in 221 B.C. he became <u>the first emperor of China.</u>

3. Ch'in Shih Huang Ti built the Great Wall to keep <u>barbarians from attacking</u> <u>China from the north.</u>

4. Because Ch'in Shih Huang Ti <u>became so afraid that someone would kill him,</u> he traveled constantly.

5. To guard his spirit, the emperor <u>had workers make thousands of clay "spirit"</u> <u>soldiers and horses for his tomb.</u>

6. The Chinese are taking a long time to excavate, or dig out, the tomb of the first emperor because <u>they need more trained archaeologists.</u>

Advice to the First Emperor

7. Hanfeizi agreed with Li Si's advice to Ch'in Shih Huang Ti — a ruler should <u>force people to obey with strict rules and punishments.</u>

Ancient Chinese Art

Use the context to help you define the italicized words in each group of sentences below. Then answer the questions that follow.

1. The historians learned about the ancient culture from the records archaeologists discovered. Apparently, the *artisans* formed a community of craftsmen and craftswomen in the small village by the sea. They felt they could encourage and help one another by living together away from a city. Their plan worked, and before long, visitors went to buy their art. The community, which had begun as a dream, *flourished* and prospered.

   (Answers will vary.)

   What do you think *artisans* are? _____

   _____

   What do you think *flourished* means? _____

   _____

2. The salesman realized he would have to increase his sales if he wanted to *surpass* his past year's income. He developed a *practical* plan. He went to all his neighbors and asked them to suggest new customers in neighboring towns. He planned to *compute* exactly how many new customers he would need to reach his goal after he had a long list of names.

   (Answers will vary.)

   What do you think *surpass* means? _____

   _____

   What do you think *practical* means? _____

   _____

   What do you think *compute* means? _____

   _____

3. In the village long, long ago, the people had no way to keep track of hours and days. One gifted inventor announced a dream in which he had seen a box with a *pendulum* swinging regularly inside. He believed the box would somehow solve the villagers' problems, but he couldn't quite figure out how. He stayed up for many days to solve the problem, and it was only when he developed a *tremor* that he could convince himself to rest.

   (Answers will vary.)

   What do you think a *pendulum* is? _____

   _____

   What do you think a *tremor* is? _____

   _____

Ancient Chinese Art

Write the answer to each question below. Look back at the selection if you need help.

Science in Ancient China

Silk

1. When did the Chinese learn how to raise silkworms and weave silk? <u>No one really knows; legends say in 2640 B.C.</u>

2. What are some labor-saving machines the Chinese invented to help the silk weavers? <u>looms, spinning wheels, water wheels, and weaving machines</u>

Porcelain and Bronze

3. Why has Chinese white clay porcelain been considered so beautiful? <u>It is so thin and delicate that light can shine through it.</u>

4. What metals did the Chinese combine to make bronze? <u>copper and tin</u>

From Steel to Seismographs

5. What is one use the Chinese discovered for steel? <u>steel bits for drilling wells</u>

6. How did Chang Hêng's seismograph indicate an earthquake? <u>A copper ball dropped from a metal dragon's mouth when a quake was felt.</u>

Kites and Balloons

7. Why were Chinese kites useful in warfare? <u>They were used to signal or to frighten the enemy.</u>

8. How did the Chinese use hot air balloons? <u>to float overhead at special celebrations</u>

The Perfection of Art in China

9. In Abu Zeid al Hasan's story, what realistic detail did the artist forget to show? <u>The bird's weight should bend the ear of corn.</u>

Sons of the Steppe

The entry words and sample sentences are missing from these definitions. Complete each definition by writing the correct entry word and a sample sentence.

eerie	astrologer	dumbfounded	err
incited	singed	contemptuously	spellbound

err

To make a mistake or error; be incorrect: **(Answers will vary.)**

_____

_____

eerie

Inspiring fear without being openly threatening; strangely unsettling; weird: _____

_____

astrologer

One who predicts the course of human events through the study of the positions of the stars and planets: _____

_____

spellbound

Held as if under a spell or a charm; fascinated; astonished: _____

_____

dumbfounded

Made speechless with astonishment; stunned: _____

_____

contemptuously

In a way that suggests that someone or something is inferior and undesirable: _____

_____

singed

Burned off (as of feathers, bristles, or hair) by being held to a flame: _____

_____

incited

Provoked (as of an action); stirred up; urged on: _____

_____

_____

Sons of the Steppe

Before Reading   Recall what you inferred about the characters and setting of "Sons of the Steppe," and keep these things in mind as you read the selection.

Read pages 234–239.   As you read to the break on page 239, notice the way historical fiction brings history to life. Then come back to this page and explain the key event below.   (Sample answers)

Key event	Explanation of event	Result of event
An eclipse of the moon occurs.	**The khan threatens to kill Yeliu if the eclipse he has predicted does not take place. After the eclipse begins, the khan sets Yeliu free.**	Yeliu joins the khan's service.

Read pages 239–246, noticing key events and what happens in the plot as a result of them. Then come back to this page and explain the events below.

Key event	Explanation of event	Result of event
Tang Liweng is taken prisoner.	**Tang Liweng despises his former student Yeliu for serving the khan. Tang Liweng would rather die than serve the conqueror of the Chinese people.**	**Tang Liweng is taken away, probably to his death.**
The phoenix predicts Kublai's future.	**Someday Kublai will rule the khan's empire.**	**Yeliu becomes Kublai's teacher.**

After Reading   Can you answer the *Thinking and Discussing* questions on page 247? If not, reread the selection, using the Stop and Think Strategy as needed.

Sons of the Steppe

Complete the story map below. Look back at the story if you need help.

Setting (pages 234–241)
the steppe, Genghis Khan's yurt

Main characters Genghis Khan, the sage Yeliu

Minor characters Chepe, Arik-Buka, Tang Liweng, Kublai

Plot

Beginning (pages 235–239)
Genghis Khan does not trust Yeliu when he predicts an eclipse of the moon.
When Yeliu is right, the Khan asks him to dinner.

Middle (pages 240–243)   Tang Liweng, a scholar, is captured. He insults Yeliu and the Khan. The Khan orders his men to destroy Tang Liweng.

Climax (pages 244–245)   The Khan believes Yeliu when he foretells that Kublai will rule the world and says that the bird Phoenix entered the yurt and touched his beak only to Kublai.

Conclusion (page 246)   The Khan assigns Yeliu to teach Kublai his knowledge.

Use the information from your story map to retell the story to someone who hasn't read it.

Kublai Khan: Eyewitness Accounts

In each group of words below, draw a line through the word that does not belong in the group, and then explain how the other three words do belong together.

(Sample answers)

vessel   suitcase   box   ~~garage~~
All words except *garage* name containers that you can carry.

fabricated   manufactured   ~~imagined~~   fashioned
All words except *imagined* mean "made."

resides   ~~visits~~   dwells   inhabits
All words except *visits* refer to living in a place.

abundance   affluence   bonanza   ~~skimpiness~~
All words except *skimpiness* mean "plenty."

remitted   ~~resumed~~   halted   canceled
All words except *resumed* mean "stopped, suspended, or canceled."

~~hidden~~   extent   expanse   length
All words except *hidden* refer to an area or a size.

threshold   ~~window~~   sill   base
All words except *window* refer to the bottom part of an object.

tribute   contribution   ~~receipt~~   wages
All words except *receipt* represent money being paid or given.

offence   crime   felony   ~~officer~~
All words except *officer* refer to acts that are against the law.

Suppose you are an explorer in thirteenth-century China. Use the vocabulary words to describe your experiences.

_____

_____

_____

_____

_____

Kublai Khan: Eyewitness Accounts

Before Reading Recall what you expected to find out by reading "Kublai Khan," and keep those things in mind as you read the selections.

Read "The Great Khan." As you read, notice the facts observed by Marco Polo. Then come back to this page and write down the inferences you make from the facts below.

(Sample answers)

Fact	Inference
Each empress has a palace and three hundred attendants.	The khan is very wealthy.
On festival days, the khan sits above everyone else.	The khan is expressing his power and superiority.
Foreign merchants must use the khan's paper money.	This clever policy has made the khan wealthy.
The khan preserves grain for use in calamities.	The khan protects his people from hunger.
There are strict rules of behavior in the khan's residence.	The khan demands respect for himself and his palace.

Read "The Land of China." Notice the facts about life in China. Then come back to this page and write down what you infer about the khan's government from the facts below.

The Chinese are highly skilled in growing crops, making pottery, and painting portraits.	The people are very productive, so they probably have a good government.

After Reading Can you answer the *Thinking and Discussing* questions on page 255? If not, reread the selections, using the Stop and Think Strategy as needed.

Kublai Khan: Eyewitness Accounts

Complete each incomplete sentence below. Look back at the selection if you need help.

The Great Khan   (Sample answers)

1. The all-powerful Great Khan lives in great splendor.

   Details

   a. When the Khan holds court on a feast day, his table is higher than all the rest.

   _____

   b. When the Khan drinks, his cupbearer and everyone present kneel.

   _____

2. The Great Khan prints paper money made from mulberry tree bark.

   Details

   a. If anyone coins or uses any other money in the kingdom, he or she is killed.

   b. The Khan uses paper money to pay the salaries and wages of his army, households and courtiers.

3. The Khan is responsible for the condition of his empire. If any part of the empire has poor crops, he cancels the taxes for one year and sends the hungry people food and seed grain.

   _____

The Land of China

4. Ibn Battuta writes that no other country can produce the equal of China's produce, porcelain, silk, and gold and silver.

5. Rich and poor Chinese wear the same kind of clothing, and silk is so cheap that even the very poorest wear it.

6. The Chinese are skillful in the arts and portraiture.

   Details

   a. In one evening, artists paint perfect likenesses of Ibn Battuta and his companions.

   b. Any stranger who commits a crime is caught because his portrait is sent all over China.

Comparing and Contrasting Sources of Information

Read the following selection from a social studies textbook about the Qing dynasty. Then answer the questions.

The Qing Dynasty

The Ming ruler sent armies to the south to fight the peasants who were rebelling. A tribal people from the north, known as the Manchus, seized this opportunity to invade northern China. In 1644, they defeated the Ming and began the Qing (pronounced *ching*) dynasty, which was to last until 1912.

Like the Mongols, the Manchus wanted to keep their tribal traditions. Control of the army was kept in Manchu hands. For governing their subjects, however, the Qing adopted Chinese traditions. The Manchus continued the Ming government structure and civil service system. They even allowed many Ming officials to remain in office. Positions in the local government were filled mostly by Chinese rather than Manchu officials.

Culture and Population

The Qing rulers also assigned scholars to edit Chinese literary and historical works, including the Confucian classics. The large-scale shift from woodblock printing to movable type in the 1500's triggered a boom in publishing and a rising literacy rate. In 1726, a famous encyclopedia of 5020 volumes was completed. Of course, a volume of entries written in Chinese characters takes up far more pages than the same entries written in English.

The population of China was about 60 million in 1400. By 1580, it had more than tripled, and it continued to increase rapidly during the Qing dynasty. By 1850, the population was about 430 million. This population growth was caused in part by the nutritious foods introduced during the Ming dynasty. As the population grew, China's territory also increased. During the Qing dynasty, China doubled in size, expanding north into Manchuria and Mongolia, west into Tibet, and south into what is now Burma and Vietnam.

1. Describe the difference between primary sources and secondary sources.

   (Sample answers)

   Primary sources are documents from the past, including diaries, letters, speeches, eyewitness accounts, poetry, literature, paintings, and artifacts; they are of the historical period. Secondary sources are books and articles about historical events written after the events they describe occurred; they are based on research into the period.

2. What kind of source is the textbook account of the Qing dynasty?

   a secondary source

3. In the opening section, what primary sources do you think the author might use to confirm information about the Manchus? What secondary sources?

   Primary sources might include official records, artwork, and accounts by observers of the time. Secondary sources would include history books written after the Qing dynasty.

4. In the section on "Culture and Population," what primary source is referred to directly, though not quoted? What information is given about this source?

   The encyclopedia of 1726. It was printed with movable type and had 5020 volumes.

5. What might a quotation from this source contribute to the selection?

   It would give a reader a sense of the type of information in the encyclopedia as well as of the style of the authors.

6. What primary sources might have provided the information about the population of China during the Qing dynasty?

   Birth records, census reports, and other official records might provide such information.

History Writing: Chronological Divisions; Art and Technology

Read the following social studies selection about Emperor Wen, who reunited the Chinese Empire. Then answer the questions.

The Reunification of China

A northern offical named Yang Jian seized power and declared himself emperor of northern China in A.D. 581 and then conquered the south by 589. Yang Jian's title was Emperor Wen, and the dynasty he founded is known as the Sui (pronounced *sway*) dynasty.

A National Identity

Emperor Wen's greatest challenge was to reverse the forces that divided China. He used several techniques to do this. For one thing, he followed ancient Chinese political practices. For example, when his supporters proclaimed him emperor, he accepted the traditional imperial gifts, including red doors for his house and a robe with a red sash — but only after he had refused them three times, as tradition demanded. By following such ancient traditions, the emperor reminded his people of their common history.

Like emperors of the Han dynasty, Emperor Wen organized public works projects. These projects focused people's attention on the common goals of the empire. Using forced-labor crews, the emperor built a grand capital city at Changan. He also oversaw the rebuilding of the Great Wall, which had been built after 214 B.C., to protect China from the central Asian nomads who continued to attack the north.

During Emperor Wen's reign, workers began work on the Grand Canal between the Huang He, formerly called the Yellow River, and the Chang Jiang. After the Grand Canal opened in 605, it transported government officials, grain, and silk.

Scholarship had been important in earlier Chinese society. Emperor Wen renewed this tradition by founding colleges for the study of the classics. He also set up schools for learning calligraphy, or the writing of Chinese characters, and for accounting and law. Since many ancient manuscripts had been lost after the fall of the Han dynasty, Emperor Wen collected books from throughout the empire. Scholars organized and classified the texts; then clerks copied them by hand. In this way, Emperor Wen ensured the preservation of the Chinese classics.

1. What chronological period began in A.D. 581? _the beginning of the Sui dynasty_

2. What subheading might be added immediately under "The Reunification of China"? _"The Sui Dynasty"_

3. Would you term the organization of the selection's material chronological? Explain.
   Yes, the information is organized chronologically. The selection is concerned
   mainly with a specific period of Chinese history and the changes that took place
   within that period.

4. What features of Chinese life provide the main focus of the chronological period that is discussed in the second, third, and fourth paragraphs?
   government-sponsored building projects, scholarship, and literature

5. What public works projects did Emperor Wen undertake?
   building the grand capital at Changan, rebuilding the Great Wall, and building the
   Grand Canal

6. How did Emperor Wen's public works projects affect the Chinese people?
   They focused the people's attention on the common goals of the empire and
   contributed to their safety, prosperity, and well-being.

7. How did Emperor Wen renew the tradition of scholarship?
   by founding colleges; by setting up schools of calligraphy, law, and accounting;
   and by preserving Chinese classics

BOOK 4

Figurative Language

Walt Whitman wrote "O Captain! My Captain!" as a tribute to Abraham Lincoln upon his assassination by John Wilkes Booth. Lincoln's leadership had been responsible for the Union victory in the Civil War and for reuniting the divided nation.

Read the poem. Then answer the questions.

O Captain! My Captain!

by Walt Whitman

O Captain! my Captain! our fearful trip is done,
The ship has weather'd every rack, the prize we sought is won,
The port is near, the bells I hear, the people all exulting,
While follow eyes the steady keel, the vessel grim and daring;
    But O heart! heart! heart!
      O the bleeding drops of red,
        Where on the deck my Captain lies,
          Fallen cold and dead.

O Captain! my Captain! rise up and hear the bells;
Rise up — for you the flag is flung — for you the bugle trills,
For you bouquets and ribbon'd wreaths — for you the shores
   a-crowding,
For you they call, the swaying mass, the eager faces turning;
    Here captain! dear father!
      The arm beneath your head!
        It is some dream that on the deck,
          You've fallen cold and dead.

My Captain does not answer, his lips are pale and still,
My father does not feel my arm, he has no pulse nor will.
The ship is anchor'd safe and sound, its voyage closed and
   done,
From fearful trip the victor ship comes in with object won;
    Exult O shores, and ring O bells!
      But I with mournful tread,
        Walk the deck my Captain lies,
          Fallen cold and dead.

Give a brief description of each of the following comparisons, all of which are forms of figurative language.

Simile A simile sets up a comparison using the words *like* or *as*.

Metaphor A metaphor is a comparison that states that one thing *is* another thing.

Personification A personification is a comparison in which human qualities or characteristics are attributed to animals or things.

Find the metaphor in the first verse. What things are compared? The United States is compared to a ship.

What does the long, difficult voyage of the ship represent? The voyage is a metaphor for the Civil War.

Change the metaphor of the war as a voyage into a simile by completing this sentence.

The Civil War was like a long, difficult voyage.

Find an example of personification in the first verse. Explain the effect the personification has on the poem.

(Sample answer) The vessel, which is a metaphor for the nation, is said to be "grim and daring." Here Whitman is attributing human qualities to the ship/nation. The effect on the poem is to reinforce the idea of the difficult voyage/war that has been endured; it helps create an image of someone or something that possesses determination and courage.

What does the "prize" refer to in the first verse? The "prize" refers to the Union victory and the reunification of the United States.

In the second verse, the poet uses the image of bouquets and ribbons to express a sad irony. On the one hand, they stand for the victory celebration of the people "who are crowding the shores." What else might they stand for?

They might also stand for the flowers and ribbons that will be placed on Lincoln's grave.

The ship is a metaphor for the nation; the voyage is a metaphor for the war. What is the third metaphor on which the poem is built?

The "Captain" of the ship is Abraham Lincoln, the president of the country.

Rhyme, Rhythm, Repetition

Read the poem by Emily Dickinson. Then answer the questions.

Autumn

The morns are meeker than they were,
The nuts are getting brown;
The berry's cheek is plumper,
The rose is out of town.

The maple wears a gayer scarf,
The field a scarlet gown.
Lest I should be old-fashioned,
I'll put a trinket on.

Why do you think poets use the techniques of rhyme, rhythm, and repetition? **(Sample answer) Poets use the techniques to help images come alive and to help the reader understand and enjoy the poem.**

Which words rhyme at the ends of lines in the first verse? **brown, town**

In the second verse, the words at the ends of the second and fourth lines form a kind of "forced" rhyme. What is the effect on the poem of this forced rhyme? **(Answers will vary, but students may point out that the effect is humorous, reinforcing the lighthearted intention of the final image: the poet dressing up like Mother Nature.)**

Would you describe the rhyme pattern overall as regular or irregular? **(Sample answer) The rhyme pattern is generally regular. That regularity helps the humor of the last line — the poet is writing playfully against the rhyme pattern she has set up.**

How would you describe the rhythm of the poem? Is it regular or irregular? **The rhythm is generally regular.**

Now read the following poem by William H. Davies. Then answer the questions.

What is this life if, full of care,
We have no time to stand and stare?

No time to stand beneath the boughs
And stare as long as sheep or cows.

No time to see, when woods we pass,
Where squirrels hide their nuts in grass.

No time to see, in broad daylight,
Streams full of stars, like skies at night.

No time to turn at Beauty's glance,
And watch her feet, how they can dance.

No time to wait till her mouth can
Enrich that smile her eyes began.

A poor life this if, full of care,
We have no time to stand and stare.

Would you describe the rhyme pattern as regular or irregular? It is regular, made up of two-line verses that rhyme.

Would you describe the rhythm as regular or irregular? It is regular.

What examples of repetition do you see in the poem? The phrase *no time* appears seven times.

What is the message of the poem? The message of the poem is that people should take time out of their busy lives to appreciate nature and the world around them.

What effect does the repetition have on the message of the poem? (Sample answer) Five of the verses begin with *No time,* forcefully reminding the reader of how busy people can be — one can almost see a busy person saying, "I have no time, no time, no time" to enjoy nature. The poet has created an ironic image to express his message.

What other example of near repetition can you find at the beginning and end of the poem? The wordings of the first verse and the last verse are very close. The first verse asks a question, and the last verse answers it.

BOOK 5

Boris

ruefully	ominous	bewildering	reluctant
menacing	pondered	indecisively	interpreter
desolate	humanity	indignantly	inhumane
drone			

Think about the meanings of the words in the box. Complete the paragraphs below by writing the correct words in the blanks.

We had been lost for six days. We hadn't seen another person or a house in all that time. The _____desolate_____ landscape filled us with dread. To make matters worse, threatening clouds were _____menacing_____. Our _____ominous_____ situation promised trouble and danger. We set up a temporary camp and _____pondered_____ our chances.

Unable to reach a conclusion about what to do, we responded _____indecisively_____ to all the _____bewildering_____ questions facing us. Should we keep walking? Should we stay in our camp and wait for help? Most of us were _____reluctant_____ to leave the camp, and we responded _____indignantly_____ to suggestions that we were cowards. I yelled without a trace of _____humanity_____ at a close friend who wanted to leave. Sorry about how _____inhumane_____ I sounded, I apologized _____ruefully_____ and explained that I was really afraid.

After an hour of discussion, we all agreed to wait in the camp. Two days later, the sun came out, and early in the afternoon, we heard the _____drone_____ of a helicopter. People were searching for us! The helicopter landed. The rescuers who ran toward us didn't speak English, but we didn't need an _____interpreter_____ to let them know how relieved we were.

Boris

Complete each incomplete sentence below. Look back at the selection if you need help.

1. Boris and Nadia are starving because <u>the German army has surrounded their city.</u>

2. The two young people try to <u>find potatoes hidden in a field.</u>

3. Crossing under the bridge is almost impossible for Boris, and he is amazed because <u>Nadia seems so brave.</u>

4. When Nadia collapses, Boris forgets his fear because he knows <u>Nadia's life depends on him.</u>

5. Boris tries to scare the German soldier with his unloaded revolver so that <u>the soldier won't think a Russian is afraid.</u>

6. Boris gladly accepts the German's chocolate because <u>he knows from his own experience that these soldiers are friendly.</u>

7. When the Russians come, Boris tries to <u>protect the German officer by standing in front of him.</u>

8. The Russian lieutenant thanks the Germans for returning Boris and Nadia by <u>saluting the German officer.</u>

Escape to Freedom

ignorant	emotions	contradict
vehemently	tentative	reluctantly

Write each word from the box above on the line next to its correct definition.

contradict   To assert or express the opposite of

tentative   Not certain or permanent

ignorant   Without education or knowledge

reluctantly   In an unwilling manner

emotions   Strong, complicated feelings

vehemently   Marked by forcefulness of expression or intensity of emotions or feelings

Now use the words from the box to complete the chart below. Then use the antonyms of the italicized words as you complete the sentences following the chart.

Synonym	Vocabulary Word	Antonym
oppose	contradict	agree
uncertain	tentative	definite
forcefully	vehemently	calmly
unknowing	ignorant	knowledgeable
hesitantly	reluctantly	willingly
feelings	emotions	ideas

1. Most of the players *willingly* go to practice, but _(Answers will vary but should contain the word *reluctantly*.)_

2. The organizers of the party say all of the arrangements for entertainment are *definite*, but _(Answers will vary but should contain the word *tentative*.)_

3. The panelists listened *calmly* to all of the questions, but _(Answers will vary but should contain the word *vehemently*.)_

Escape to Freedom

Before Reading   Recall your prediction about "Escape to Freedom," and keep it in mind as you read the selection.

Read pages 329–336.   As you read, notice details that reveal Fred's inner conflict about being a slave. Then come back to this page and make notes below about details that reveal the conflicts.

(Sample answers)

A slave's proper behavior Fred hears conflicting opinions. Jethro says Fred should keep his head bowed and his eyes on the ground, and he should do whatever he is told right away with no back talk. Mrs. Auld says we are all God's children, and Fred mustn't bow to her. Mr. Auld says that a slave is not human and does not have a soul.	**A slave learning to read** Mrs. Auld begins to teach Fred to read. Mr. Auld forbids this as unlawful and unsafe. Fred realizes that white people have enslaved blacks by keeping them ignorant.

Read pages 337–341, noticing details that reveal Fred's struggle of conscience. Then come back to this page and make notes about the situations below.

Fred questions white people's ideas. Fred challenges Mrs. Auld about why she won't teach him to read. He asks Robert whether slavery is fair.	**Fred tries to learn to read.** Mrs. Auld forbids Fred to learn to read, but he is determined. He persuades Robert to teach him in exchange for food.

After Reading   Can you answer the *Thinking and Discussing* questions on page 342? If not, reread the selection, using the Stop and Think Strategy as needed.

Escape to Freedom

The events in the box are out of order. Write them in the correct sequence on the lines that follow.

> Fred realizes that slavery is harmful to the slaveowner as well as the slave.
>
> Mrs. Auld tells Fred that God makes no difference between a slave and a master, and starts to teach Fred to read.
>
> Robert starts teaching Fred when Fred explains that as soon as he learns to read he'll be free.
>
> Fred figures out that education and being able to read will make him free.

1. White Woman — Sophia Auld — tells White Boy — her son, Thomas — to read for Fred.

2. When Thomas refuses to read, Fred tries to figure out what the Bible says.

3. **Mrs. Auld tells Fred that God makes no difference between a slave and a master, and starts to teach Fred to read.**

4. White Man — Hugh Auld — forbids his wife to teach Fred, telling her that it is unlawful and unsafe and makes slaves unhappy.

5. **Fred figures out that education and being able to read will make him free.**

6. When Fred asks Mrs. Auld why it's against the law for her to teach him how to read, she tells him to get out.

7. **Fred realizes that slavery is harmful to the slaveowner as well as the slave.**

8. Fred makes friends with a poor white boy — Robert — so that Robert will teach him to read.

9. **Robert starts teaching Fred when Fred explains that as soon as he learns to read he'll be free.**

10. When Mrs. Auld tears up Robert's book, Fred picks up the torn pages, opens the book, and begins to read.

Dicey's Song

confident	conflict	deceitfulness
impassive	liable	resent

Imagine that you are a reporter for a school newspaper. For the next issue, you are going to interview a new student. Write the answers that a new student might give you. In each answer, be sure to use a word from the box that has the same meaning as the italicized words in the question.

Some of your friends have told me that you moved to this town very suddenly. Do you *feel angry or bitter about* leaving your other home without much warning? (Answers will vary but should contain the word *resent.*)
_____

We've heard that you enjoyed sports at your old school. What teams are you *likely* to try out for here? (Answers will vary but should contain the word *liable.*)

We've also heard that you are a great student who likes most classes. Do your athletic interests ever *clash* with your academic ones? (Answers will vary but should contain the word *conflict.*)

In your first few days here, you looked very *calm* and *didn't show much emotion.* Did you really feel calm, or was it scary to come to a new school? (Answers will vary but should contain the word *impassive.*)
_____

Would you say you feel more *sure of yourself* now? (Answers will vary but should contain the word *confident.*)

What would you tell people about your values and feelings about *making others believe things that aren't true*? (Answers will vary but should contain the word *deceitfulness.*)

Dicey's Song

Before Reading   Recall your prediction about "Dicey's Song," and keep it in mind as you read the selection.

Read pages 345–352.   As you read to the end of the essay on page 352, think about the tone of each student's essay. For example, the tone might be cheerful, confident, or sad. Then come back to this page and make notes below about the essays.   (Sample answers)

Tone of Mina's essay and what it reveals about Mina (pages 348–350)

The tone is forthright and honest. It shows self-awareness and self-confidence. It also shows Mina's cleverness in writing about herself.

Tone of Dicey's essay and what it reveals about Dicey (pages 351–352)

The tone is quiet and sensitive to the unhappiness of Mrs. Liza. It shows Dicey's sympathy, respect, and love for her.

Read pages 352–361, noticing how the author changes the tone in describing the characters' words and actions. Then come back to this page and make notes below about the tone.

Tone of Mr. Chappelle's accusation of plagiarism (page 355)

The tone is accusing and suspicious. Mr. Chappelle is totally confident that he is right.

Tone of Dicey's thought about sailing the little boat (page 357)

The tone is quiet, soothing, and comforting. The thought is her way of escaping from an embarrassing situation.

After Reading   Can you answer the *Thinking and Discussing* questions on page 362? If not, reread the selection, using the Stop and Think Strategy as needed.

Dicey's Song

Write each plot element and event where it belongs in the diagram. See if you agree or disagree with the two completed boxes.

Event   Mr. Chappelle accuses Dicey of plagiarism.

Event   Mina compliments Dicey.

Plot element   Gram helps Dicey laugh at what happened at school.

Event   Mr. Chappelle reads Dicey's essay.

Plot element   Mina proves that Mr. Chappelle is wrong when she gets Dicey to admit she wrote the essay and that she knows Mrs. Liza.

Event   When Mr. Chappelle reads Mina's essay, Dicey is surprised by how good it is.

Problem

Dicey wants to find out her grade — whether her essay is as good as she thinks it is.

Plot

Rising action: Events

1.   Event: When Mr. Chappelle reads Mina's essay, Dicey is surprised by how good it is.

2.   Event: Mr. Chappelle reads Dicey's essay.

3.   Event: Mina compliments Dicey.

4.   Event: Mr. Chappelle accuses Dicey of plagiarism.

Climax

Mina proves that Mr. Chappelle is wrong when she gets Dicey to admit she wrote the essay and that she knows Mrs. Liza.

Falling action

Mr. Chappelle apologizes and says he'll give Dicey an A+.

Conclusion

Gram helps Dicey laugh at what happened at school.

Jeremiah's Song

The word in the center of each word web appears in "Jeremiah's Song." Complete the webs by filling in the circles with the following words and phrases: *conclusion, turned backward, reverse, disease, change, illness.* Add more circles for other words you associate with the center word.

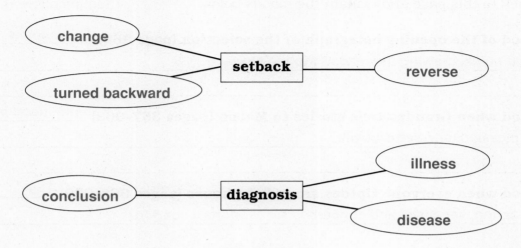

Now use the words from each web in a brief description of how a diagnosis might cause a setback.

_____

_____

_____

_____

_____

_____

_____

_____

_____

_____

_____

_____

_____

_____

Jeremiah's Song

Before Reading   Recall your predictions about "Jeremiah's Song," and keep them in mind as you read the selection.

Read pages 366–369.   As you read, notice the way the author presents a variety of moods to show the characters' feelings. Then come back to this page and explain the moods below.   (Sample answers)

The mood of the opening paragraph of the selection (page 366) The mood is bright and quick, drawing the reader into the story.

_____

The mood when Grandpa tells stories to Macon (pages 367–368) The mood is relaxed, pleasant, and comfortable.

_____

The mood when everyone tiptoes around the house (pages 368–369) The mood is caring, sensitive, and concerned for Grandpa's comfort.

_____

Read pages 370–375, noticing changing moods in the story. Then come back to this page and explain the moods below.

The mood of Grandpa's story about Old Carrie (page 370) The mood is creepy, scary, and spine-chilling.

_____

The mood when Ellie describes the stories as "a secret language" (page 372) The mood is questioning and speculating.

_____

The mood when Macon plays the guitar at the graveyard (pages 374–375) The mood is very sad as they leave Grandpa in the graveyard.

_____

After Reading   Can you answer the *Thinking and Discussing* questions on page 376? If not, reread the selection, using the Stop and Think Strategy as needed.

Jeremiah's Song

Write the answer to each question below. Look back at the selection if you need help.

(Sample answers)

1. How has Cousin Ellie changed after her first year of college? Ellie thinks Grandpa Jeremiah's old-fashioned; she doesn't want to hear his stories anymore because she thinks he makes them up.

2. How did the narrator feel before and how does he feel now about Grandpa Jeremiah's stories? At first the narrator liked to hear the stories, but now they scare him.

3. Why does Macon start helping with the chores and listening to Grandpa Jeremiah's stories? Macon wants to help Grandpa Jeremiah, who may not live long; he also thinks the stories are important.

4. How is Grandpa Jeremiah's health when Ellie comes home from college again? He is very ill.

5. Why is Ellie angry when Macon encourages Grandpa Jeremiah to tell his old stories? Ellie says that Macon is tiring Grandpa Jeremiah, but she may feel the stories are outdated.

6. What is Ellie's answer when the narrator asks her why she is upset with Dr. Crawford? They have to get away from the kind of life that keeps them in the past.

7. How can the narrator tell that Macon and Ellie have become friends at last? Ellie gives Macon a dish of pork chops without his asking her.

8. What does Grandpa Jeremiah say when the narrator says that Ellie thinks he and Macon are talking about something more than the stories? In hard times, it helps to know what people who lived long ago went through without giving up.

9. When the narrator listens to Macon's tune, what does he think he might be able to do some day? He can learn Macon's tune if he wants.

Using Details to Understand Character Development

Read the following excerpt from "The Sentimentality of William Tavener" by Willa Cather. Then answer the questions.

One spring night Hester sat in a rocking chair by the sitting room window, darning socks. She rocked violently and sent her long needle vigorously back and forth over her gourd, and it took only a very casual glance to see that she was wrought up over something. William sat on the other side of the table reading his farm paper. If he had noticed his wife's agitation, his calm, clean-shaven face betrayed no sign of concern. He must have noticed the sarcastic turn of her remarks at the supper table, and he must have noticed the moody silence of the older boys as they ate. When supper was but half over, little Billy, the youngest, had suddenly pushed back his plate and slipped away from the table, manfully trying to swallow a sob. But William Tavener never heeded ominous forecasts in the domestic horizon, and he never looked for a storm until it broke.

After supper the boys had gone to the pond under the willows in the big cattle corral, to get rid of the dust of plowing. Hester could hear an occasional splash and a laugh ringing clear through the stillness of the night, as she sat by the open window. She sat silent for almost an hour reviewing in her mind many plans of attack. But she was too vigorous a woman to be much of a strategist, and she usually came to her point with directness. At last she cut her thread and suddenly put her darning down, saying emphatically:

"William, I don't think it would hurt you to let the boys go to that circus in town tomorrow."

William continued to read his farm paper, but it was not Hester's custom to wait for an answer. She usually divined his arguments and assailed them one by one before he uttered them.

"You've been short of hands all summer, and you've worked the boys hard, and a man ought use his own flesh and blood as well as he does his hired hands. We're plenty able to afford it, and it's little enough our boys ever spend. I don't see how you can expect 'em to be steady and hard workin', unless you encourage 'em a little. I never could see much harm in circuses, and our boys have never been to one. Oh, I know Jim Howley's boys . . . carry on when they go, but our boys ain't that sort, an' you know it, William. The animals are real instructive, an' our boys don't get to see much out here on the prairie. It was different where we were raised but the boys have got no advantages here, an' if you don't take care, they'll grow up to be greenhorns."

1. What details in the first paragraph describe Hester's actions and words? **(Sample answers)**

    She rocked violently; she sent her needle vigorously back and forth; she made

    sarcastic remarks.

    What do these details reveal about Hester's feelings?
    She is upset and angry, and having trouble concealing her feelings.

2. What details in the first paragraph describe William and his actions?
    He sat reading his paper; his calm face showed no sign of concern.

    What might these details reveal about William?
    He may not be sympathetic to his wife's feelings; he may be trying to avoid an

    argument with her.

3. How would you describe Hester's feelings about her sons?
    She feels they are hard-working, thrifty, and well-mannered. She is sympathetic and

    supportive, and she wants to treat them fairly.

4. What do Hester's words imply about William's attitude toward his sons?
    He seems to feel they ought to work hard without expecting a reward; he is

    reluctant to spend money just to give them pleasure.

5. Summarize the interaction between Hester and William up to this point.
    Hester is more outspoken than her husband and seems to find his calm silence

    exasperating. William seems to be trying to ignore his wife's agitation as long as

    possible to avoid conflict.

Understanding Mood and Tone

Read the next excerpt from "The Sentimentality of William Tavener" by Willa Cather. Then answer the questions.

Hester paused a moment, and William folded up his paper, but vouchsafed no remark. His sisters in Virginia had often said that only a quiet man like William could ever have lived with Hester Perkins. Secretly, William was rather proud of his wife's "gift of speech." . . .

Hester shook out another sock and went on.

"Nobody was ever hurt by goin' to a circus. Why, law me! I remember I went to one myself once, when I was little. I had most forgot about it. It was over at Pewtown, an' I remember how I had set my heart on going. I don't think I'd ever forgiven my father if he hadn't taken me, though that red clay road was in a frightful way after the rain. I mind they had an elephant and six poll parrots, and a Rocky Mountain lion, an' a cage of monkeys, an' two camels. My! but they were a sight to me then!"

Hester dropped the black sock and shook her head and smiled at the recollection. She was not expecting anything from William yet, and she was fairly startled when he said gravely . . .

"No, there was only one camel.

The other was a dromedary."

She peered around the lamp and looked at him keenly.

"Why, William, how come you to know?"

William folded his paper and answered with some hesitation, "I was there, too."

Hester's interest flashed up. "Well, I never, William! To think of my finding it out after all these years! Why, you couldn't have been much bigger'n our Billy then. It seems queer I never saw you when you was little, to remember about you. But then you Back Creek folks never have anything to do with us Gap people. But how come you to go? Your Father was stricter with you than you are with your boys."

"I reckon I shouldn't 'a gone," he said slowly, "but boys will do foolish things. . . . I slipped off unbeknownst to father an' went to the show."

Hester spoke up warmly: "Nonsense, William! It didn't do you no harm, I guess. You was always worked hard enough. It must have been a big sight for a little fellow. That clown must have just tickled you to death."

1. What tone does the author use in the first paragraph when she describes the sisters' comment about Hester as well as William's response to it?

(Sample answers)

It is ironic.

What does this reveal about the author's feelings toward the characters?

It shows that she respects their independence, in spite of the fact that they have qualities that others might view in a negative way.

2. What shift in tone does the author introduce in the first paragraph?

The tone seems to be shifting from one of anger and conflict to one of mutual understanding.

What clue to this shift in tone does the author provide?

William is shown to be secretly proud of his wife's talkativeness, rather than resentful of it.

3. What seems to be the tone of Hester's first sentence to William in paragraph 3?

exasperation; frustration at her inability to convince him

4. By the end of paragraph 3, how has the tone of Hester's remarks changed?

She seems nostalgic, recollecting a pleasant memory from the past.

What does the tone suggest about Hester?

That she has a soft side to her character that she probably hides most of the time.

5. How does the mood change after William reveals that he, too, had been to the circus, and had gone without his father's permission?

The mood becomes lighter, friendlier, and more confidential. Earlier, Hester was arguing on her sons' behalf, but as the conversation progresses, Hester shows that she understands how hard William's childhood was, and thinks he had a right to go to the circus.

6. What words and phrases show the change in tone?

"Hester's interest flashed," "Hester spoke up warmly," "always worked hard enough," "tickled you to death"

BOOK 6

The Strange Illness of Mr. Arthur Cook

Use the words in the box below to complete the sentences. Then use the clues from the sentences to help you fill in the flow chart.

| patience | inquiries | climax | inquisitive | humor |

Like a detective, a person who is ___inquisitive___ often makes ___inquiries___ about strange situations. This type of person needs ___patience___, while persistently seeking clues, and a sense of ___humor___, to help lighten heavy hours of hard work. With these qualities and a sharp mind, such a person may solve a case before it even reaches a ___climax___.

inquisitive

↓

inquiries

patience   humor

↓

climax

Think about the relationship of the words in the flow chart. Then use it as an outline for a description of an inquisitive person or a time when you were inquisitive. Use a separate sheet of paper. Make sure you use all the words in the chart.

The Strange Illness of Mr. Arthur Cook

Before Reading   Recall your prediction about "The Strange Illness of Mr. Arthur Cook," and keep it in mind as you read the selection.

Read pages 389–404.   As you read these pages, notice any fantastic images from which you can draw inferences that something out of the ordinary is happening. Then come back to this page and make notes on the subjects below.

The inference I made from the brownish fog in front of the television set _The fog must have some fantastic explanation since Mr. Cook's vision is excellent._

Mr. Cook's illness a brownish fog, headaches, strange dreams, waking at dawn, loss of appetite, irritability, restlessness	**Judy's investigation** Judy visits Mrs. Cribble (a former owner), Mr. Biley (the real estate agent), and Mrs. Baxter (the original owner).

Read pages 405–413.   Now read the rest of the selection. Then come back to this page and make notes about the subjects below.

The inference I made from the brownish fog forming into the shape of a man _This is the ghost of Mr. Baxter in his brown waterproof._

Mrs. Baxter's explanation Mr. Baxter loved his garden and swore he would not leave it, even in death. He is haunting Mr. Cook because the garden is neglected.	**Mr. Cook's recovery** Once Mr. Cook begins gardening, his health improves. Mr. Baxter's ghost is satisfied and disappears.

After Reading   Can you answer the *Thinking and Discussing* questions on page 414? If not, reread the selection, using the Stop and Think Strategy as needed.

The Strange Illness of Mr. Arthur Cook

To review the story, fill in the missing cause or effect in each item.

1. **Cause:** Southcroft is for sale very cheaply.

   Effect: The Cooks buy Southcroft.

2. **Cause:** Judy suspects that there must be something wrong with the house because Mr. Biley is so pleased when the Cooks decide to buy it.

   Effect: Judy asks Mr. Biley about the former owners.

3. **Cause:** Mr. Cook tries to watch daytime or early evening TV instead of working in the garden.

   Effect: Mr. Cook notices a brownish fog between himself and the television set.

4. **Cause:** Mr. Cook digs in the garden instead of watching television Saturday afternoon.

   Effect: His headache stops, and he can watch TV at night.

5. **Cause:** Mr. Cook has nightmares and becomes very upset.

   Effect: Judy tracks down Mrs. Baxter, a former owner.

6. **Cause:** Mrs. Baxter feels sorry for Judy and guilty about Mr. Cook's illness.

   Effect: Mrs. Baxter says Mr. Baxter is upset about his garden and won't rest.

7. **Cause:** Mrs. Cook explains to her husband that Mr. Baxter's ghost is the cause of his troubles and that he can get rid of him by fixing up the garden.

   Effect: Mr. Cook is relieved that he's not losing his mind, and he works day and night in the garden.

8. **Cause:** Mr. Cook learns to love gardening and spends every spare moment at it.

   Effect: Mr. Cook's illness is cured, he is in wonderful shape, and his family enjoys the vegetables and fruit from the garden.

Potter's Gray

Imagine that you are admiring a statue in a museum when the statue suddenly asks you some questions. In each answer, use the word from the box that means almost the same as the italicized phrase in the question.

resist	compelled	inconspicuously
outrage	fragments	detested

I often feel that I'm displayed *in a manner not very noticeable or obvious,* so what in particular made you stop to look at me in the first place? **(Answers will vary.) inconspicuously**

_____

After you noticed me, what made you feel almost *forced* to stop and study me for so long? **compelled**

_____

_____

Since you barely looked at the other art in this room, I wondered if there was anything you *disliked strongly* about it. **detested**

_____

_____

As a museum visitor, do you ever feel frustration or *deep anger* about the lack of appreciation of art? **outrage**

_____

_____

Centuries ago, I was discovered in *many pieces* in a storeroom, and I wonder what qualities you think the people who reassembled me needed. **fragments**

_____

Is there any particular form of art that you can't *keep yourself from* wanting to go see? **resist**

_____

_____

Potter's Gray

Before Reading   Recall your prediction about "Potter's Gray," and keep it in mind as you read the selection.

Read pages 419–425.   Suppose you were to direct a movie of the story "Potter's Gray." As you read, notice the fantastic images that would make the movie effective. Then come back to this page and describe the way you visualize each scene below.   (Sample answers)

The street scene in which Professor Bercy is injured <u>The Parisian street is</u> <u>crowded and noisy as Professor Bercy reaches for his glasses and is hit by a car.</u>

The scene in which Grig receives the cake <u>Eugène hands Grig a small box, which</u> <u>Grig looks at with suspicion as Anna thanks Eugène.</u>

Read pages 426–436.   As you read the rest of the selection, notice the fantastic images Grig and Anna see through the glasses. Then come back to this page and describe the images below.

The courtyard of the Louvre <u>Grig sees layers of time — people and objects from</u> <u>the past to the present.</u>

The scene that takes place between Grig and Gray <u>Grig holds out the apple to the</u> <u>horse, which eats it.</u>

The images in the gallery <u>The paintings come to life. People from other times walk</u> <u>through the gallery silently.</u>

Anna's view of Eugène <u>Anna sees Eugène's evil mind, screams with horror, and</u> <u>smashes the pink glasses.</u>

After Reading   Can you answer the *Thinking and Discussing* questions on page 437? If not, reread the selection, using the Stop and Think Strategy as needed.

Potter's Gray

To review the story, write a word or phrase to make each of the following statements true.

pages 419–423

1. Grig Rainborrow's baby sitter, Anna, is taking him to the Louvre to _meet her boyfriend._

2. Grig _hates_ Eugène because he calls Grig a little sheep in French.

3. When Grig sees a man hit by a car, Grig _picks up the man's glasses._

pages 424–425

4. Grig _looks for a place to leave_ Eugène's nasty little cake.

pages 428–429

5. Grig puts on the professor's glasses to see _the tree roots in the courtyard._

6. Grig sees something he will recall, and re-create, in later life when he has become _a famous painter._

7. Through the glasses, Grig can see _layers of time in the courtyard._

pages 429–430

8. Grig realizes that Eugène's cake has _pills_ in it. He _pushes the cake under a window seat._

pages 430–431

9. When Potter's Gray eats Grig's apple, Grig realizes that all the pictures in the gallery _have come to life._

page 433

10. Grig can see the workings of Eugène's brain and that Eugène _has an evil plan._

pages 434–435

11. Anna _puts on the glasses_ when Grig warns her he'll scream. She sees the inside of Eugène's head and _smashes the glasses._

page 436

12. Professor Bercy _dies from the accident._

13. The next day Grig visits his favorite picture, _Potter's Gray_, and remembers that he stroked Gray's nose only the day before.

The Parrot

Use the words to complete the sentences.

doom	pleadingly	conscience
vain	wretched	hesitated
sidled	confined	insistently

1. The parrot was _____confined_____ to her cage.

2. Polly seemed to look at me so _____pleadingly_____ that I finally let her out to fly about the room.

3. She _____hesitated_____ for only a second before whooshing out to freedom.

4. When I finally found my escaped parrot, it was cold and hungry and it looked _____wretched._____

5. The cat _____sidled_____ over to the bird feeder.

6. The eerie cry of the bird filled me with a sense of _____doom._____

7. I tried in _____vain_____ to get the bird to say my name.

8. My _____conscience_____ told me that I should have fed the animals before going to the ball game.

9. I argued _____insistently_____ that it was not my turn to clean the cage.

On the lines below, write a paragraph explaining how one should care for a bird; use as many of the vocabulary words as you can.

(Answers will vary.) _____

_____

_____

_____

_____

_____

The Parrot

Before Reading   Recall your prediction about "The Parrot," and keep it in mind as you read the selection.

Read pages 440–447.   As a reporter assigned to write the following news story, look for answers to the questions *who, what, where, when,* and *why*. Then come back to this page and make notes about the incident below.

(Sample answers)   **Local Girl Fears Wretched Bird**

Who? Anna

What? was frightened when she saw a gray parrot

Where? on Sebastian Street

When? on an October morning

Why? because she thought this parrot must be dead

What does the flashback reveal? It explains Anna's fear.

Read pages 448–455.   As you read, look for answers to the questions *who, what, where, when,* and *why*. Then come back to this page and make notes about the incident below.

Daughter Saves Mother's Life

Who? Anna

What? found her mother bleeding badly

Where? in the suburbs of London; in Bobby's room, on the floor

When? on an October morning

Why? because the gray parrot shrieked, "Go back!"

Which parts of the story seem to be real? Which are fantastic? Everything seems real except the ghostly parrot telling Anna to go back.

After Reading   Can you answer the *Thinking and Discussing* questions on page 456? If not, reread the selection, using the Stop and Think Strategy as needed.

The Parrot

To review the story, complete each statement in your own words.

pages 440–443

1. One October morning, on her way to school, Anna, the narrator, sees <u>an old parrot.</u>

2. Anna shakes with fright <u>when she sees the parrot.</u>

3. In Anna's childhood, her family took care of <u>Polly, a neighbor's gray parrot.</u>

4. When Anna tried to stroke the bird's head, Polly <u>bit Anna's finger.</u>

pages 443–447

5. When Polly's owner died, her sister Mrs. Jenkins tried to give the bird <u>to Anna</u> <u>and her family.</u>

6. When Anna's family didn't want the bird, Anna told Mrs. Jenkins her father said how cruel it was <u>to keep birds in cages.</u>

7. Although the October weather was cold, Mrs. Jenkins <u>released Polly outdoors.</u>

pages 448–453

8. Anna goes to a nearby house to <u>find someone to take care of the parrot.</u>

9. The parrot tells Anna, <u>"Go back! Go back!"</u>

10. Anna thinks the old gray parrot is <u>Polly's ghost.</u>

11. Finally Anna decides to run home; she flings open the door and hears <u>a crash</u> <u>and a scream.</u>

pages 453–455

12. When Anna finds her mother bleeding on the floor, she <u>gets Mrs. Jessop and</u> <u>dials 999.</u>

13. Although Bobby and Anna ask everyone on their street about the parrot, they <u>cannot find anyone to claim it.</u>

14. Anna's mother says she fell off the ladder through carelessness, but Anna thinks the accident was caused by <u>the noise of the slamming kitchen door.</u>

15. Anna will never know whether she saw a real parrot or <u>Polly's ghost.</u> She wonders whether Polly would have intended <u>to be kind or cruel.</u>

Your Mind Is a Mirror

Before each definition below, write the word that is defined.
Then write a sample sentence using the word.

anxiety	substantial	converse
depressed	subject	indifferent
precisely	effects	asserted
appalled	nondescript	

effects   Results; outcomes: (Answers will vary.)

_____

substantial   Considerable in importance, degree, or amount: _____

_____

precisely   Done within small limits of error or variation: _____

_____

converse   The opposite or reverse of something: _____

_____

asserted   Stated or declared positively: _____

_____

anxiety   A feeling of uneasiness and distress; worry: _____

_____

indifferent   Having no interest; not caring one way or the other: _____

_____

subject   Under the power or authority of another: _____

_____

depressed   Gloomy; low in spirits: _____

_____

nondescript   Lacking distinguishable qualities and thus

difficult to describe: _____

_____

appalled   Filled with horror and amazement: _____

_____

Your Mind Is a Mirror

To review the story, write each plot element and event where you think it belongs in the diagram. The numbers tell you the pages where you will find the answers.

Event   When Sam wakes up, he can't find the book or Simon.

Event   Sam steals a paperback book to bring happiness back to his own family.

Plot element   Sam's father smiles and speaks to him.

Event   Sam dreams that Madame Bonamy shows him how to travel in time.

Event   The book is in Greek, and Sam can't read it.

Plot element   Sam hopes he will find Simon.

Event   Sam discovers he can use his mind to travel in time.

Plot element   Sam's father's depression saddens the whole family.

Event   In his dream, Sam returns the book to Kerimos but loses his cat, Simon.

Problem

(460–462) Sam's father's depression saddens the whole family.

Events: Rising action

Kerimos

(463) Sam steals a paperback book to bring happiness back to his own family.

England

(464) The book is in Greek, and Sam can't read it.

(465–467) Sam dreams that Madame Bonamy shows him how to travel in time.

(468–469) In his dream, Sam returns the book to Kerimos but loses his cat, Simon.

(469–472) When Sam wakes up, he can't find the book or Simon.

(473–474) Sam discovers he can use his mind to travel in time.

Climax

(475) Sam's father smiles and speaks to him.

Conclusion

(475) Sam hopes he will find Simon.

Understanding Imagery

Read the following selection. Then answer the questions.

The Light in the Barn

Thirteen-year-old Gena Randolph stepped inside Grandpa Frazier's old barn. It was about half the size of her school auditorium. Surrounded by trees on three sides, the barn's interior was always shadowy even on luminous summer afternoons such as this one. At the back of the barn was a loft and a hanging rope ladder. Piles of crates and cardboard boxes leaned against the raw-wood walls along with bikes, hoes, rakes, shovels, horseshoes, and car jacks. A broken-down tractor rusted in the far left corner across from Grandpa's station wagon. Gena chewed on her lower lip. Over the years she'd been in the dark barn dozens of times with her parents but never alone until this afternoon.

The barn was quiet. A mouse skittered from a pile of hay near the tractor. Gena stood still and pushed her curly red hair off her face. Where had Grandpa Frazier stored the old fishing rod? She rubbed the back of her hand over her freckled forehead. The barn was cool, but Gena was still perspiring from her walk in the garden. Outside, one of Grandpa's hound dogs bellowed. Probably Mac chasing a rabbit.

A streak of light flashed in Gena's green eyes. Bright sunlight in the barn? Where was it coming from? She squinted and looked toward the loft. A white light sparkled across the rafters like a warning beacon at sea. She heard a soft moan, half-machine, half-animal, coming from overhead. Was it a call for help or a warning?

Gena felt her heart beating rapidly as the light brightened, flickered, and then faded like a spent candle. She took a deep breath and gazed across the barn. Her eyes lighted on a fishing rod resting against a tall wooden crate near the tractor. For a brief moment, she thought of the strange light again and then shrugged. Probably just her imagination.

Which of your senses do the sounds in the barn appeal to? Give examples of these sounds. **The sense of hearing. Examples of sounds are the skittering mouse, the bellowing dog, and the soft moan.**

What do these sounds help you to infer about the barn? Explain. **(Sample answer) Something unusual may happen. The combination of real noises with the mysterious moan gives a foreboding feeling.**

The white flashing light in the barn was "like a warning beacon at sea." What mental picture does this comparison suggest? What can you infer about the light? **(Sample answer) I think of a lighthouse light or a police car light. The light may be fantastic and may be warning Gena.**

What kinds of events do you expect after reading about the sounds and the light in the barn? **danger, adventure, and strange happenings**

Which things or events described in this selection are realistic, and which are probably fantastic? **The barn, the details about Gena, her actions and reactions, the mouse's action, and the dog's bellow all are realistic. The white light and the soft moan may be fantastic.**

How does the mixture of real and fantastic things and events make the story more believable? **The realistic parts draw the reader into the story so that the reader begins to believe in the character and setting. Then the reader is ready to accept the fantastic parts when they begin to happen.**

Understanding Foreshadowing, Flashback, and Symbolism

Read the following selection, which continues Gena's experiences. Then answer the questions.

That afternoon, Gena stood on the farmhouse porch, frowning and shaking her head. Where was the old fishing rod that she'd found in the barn this morning? Just minutes before, Gena had laid it across the wicker rocking chair when she ran inside to put a cheese sandwich, potato chips, and an apple into a bag for lunch at the pond.

Suddenly she heard a familiar crackling sound, familiar and strange, like a thin pane of glass shattering into ten thousand tiny pieces. Since Sunday, she'd heard the mysterious sound three times, each time after something had disappeared — first the rake, then the wheelbarrow, and now the fishing rod. What did the three objects have in common? For a long moment, Gena pondered this question. Slowly, a picture came into her mind: the ramshackle brown barn jam-packed with boxes of family mementos, tools, and Grandpa's old station wagon. Gena nodded her head. The rake, the wheelbarrow, and the fishing rod had all been stored in the barn. Each had disappeared.

And what about that strange, streaking light that she'd seen in the barn? Maybe it wasn't her imagination after all. Maybe none of this was.

Just then Gena recalled an odd conversation with her mother that had occurred on Saturday minutes before she boarded the jet in San Francisco for her first solo visit to New Hampshire. With a mysterious smile, her mother had told Gena that the old farmhouse and barn would be full of unforgettable adventures this summer now that Gena was thirteen. "This will be a magical summer, Gena," her mother said. "And I suspect that the next time I see you, you'll be quite a different young lady. But whatever happens, remember: Don't lose your courage or your generosity."

What clues in the first three paragraphs foreshadow future events?

What kinds of events does the foreshadowing prepare the reader for? __Words such__ __as *frowning, strange, mysterious,* and *streaking light* and events such as the__ __disappearance of the fishing rod prepare the reader for strange and mysterious__ __adventures.__

_____

_____

What are some other purposes of foreshadowing? How does foreshadowing help keep you interested in characters like Gena and what happens to them? It builds suspense, alerts me to future events, and makes me ask questions about the characters' future.

How does the flashback in the last paragraph help you learn about Gena? (Sample answer) Gena's conversation with her mother told where Gena came from and more about the circumstances of her visit to her grandfather.

How does the flashback help prepare you for strange or unusual events? Gena's mother said her summer would be magical and full of unforgettable adventures.

In this selection, the items that have disappeared — the rake, wheelbarrow, and fishing rod — are useful objects that could be symbols of the importance of everyday country life. What might the flashing white light symbolize? (Sample answer) Information. The light may not seem strange when Gena understands what is causing it.

Think about the kinds of events the author seems to be foreshadowing and hinting at in the flashback. On the lines below, write about an experience that Gena might have at Grandpa Frazier's farm. (Answers will vary.)

BOOK 7

Animal Behavior

Use the context to help you define the italicized words in each group of sentences below. Then answer the questions that follow.

1. Studying a wild animal in its *habitat* helps scientists understand the animal's needs and habits. Observation of animals in the wild also makes it possible to draw *conclusions* about their behavior. Scientists have eagerly traveled to jungles, forests, and grasslands to observe animals from apes to kangaroos in order to make *generalizations* about their eating, hunting, and sleeping habits. Finding common patterns of behavior can help scientists protect wildlife. **(Answers will vary.)**

What do you think *habitat* means? _____

_____

What do you think *conclusions* are? _____

_____

What do you think *generalizations* are? _____

_____

2. Labrador retrievers are excellent dogs to train for hunting or pleasure. If you throw a ball or a stick, the Labrador puppy's *response* will be to chase it. You can provide the same *stimulus* over and over again, and the puppy will never tire. This inborn desire to fetch is based on the dog's natural *instinct* to hunt. This breed of dog is also highly *social*, and Labrador retrievers love to please people. As a result, you can teach these dogs to respond to human *language*. By six months of age, a puppy can obey simple commands telling it to do such things as sit, fetch, or stay. **(Answers will vary.)**

What do you think *response* means? _____

_____

What do you think a *stimulus* is? _____

_____

What do you think *instinct* is? _____

_____

What do you think it means to be *social*? _____

_____

What do you think *language* is? _____

_____

3. For years, there has been *controversy* over the question of whether dogs are smarter than cats. Some people believe that dogs can be trained much more successfully than cats can because dogs seem to respond more readily to language. Other people insist that this *reasoning* is incorrect. They believe that if you pick any cat at *random*, the cat's intelligence will far exceed a dog's.

What do you think a *controversy* is? _____

_____

What do you think *reasoning* is? _____

_____

What do you think *random* means? _____

_____

4. There are many *theories* about why dinosaurs became extinct millions of years ago. Scientists speculate that among the different *factors* contributing to their extinction might have been the beginning of the Ice Age. Other factors might have been drought or disease.

What do you think *theories* are? _____

_____

What do you think *factors* are? _____

_____

Now answer the following questions.

Do you think a zoo is a suitable *habitat* for a monkey? Why or why not? (Answers will vary.)

_____

_____

_____

What *factors* might make studying animals in the wild difficult? (Answers will vary.)

_____

_____

_____

If the telephone rings and you answer it, what part of the event is called the *stimulus*? _____ the ring of the telephone _____

What is the *response*? _____ answering the telephone _____

Animal Behavior

Complete each incomplete sentence below. Look back at the selection if you need help.

Behavior and Learning   (Sample answers)

1. The different ways that animals react to their environments are called *behaviors*. Common animal behaviors are ___eating, home building, and sleeping.___ _____

2. Something that happens in an animal's environment is called a *stimulus*. The stimulus of danger causes animals to ___try to protect themselves.___ _____

3. All organisms are born knowing certain inborn behaviors, such as how to breathe. An inborn behavior is called a *reflex* if your body ___does it automatically.___ _____

4. More complex inborn behaviors, such as ___mating, migrating, and nest building___ _____, are called *instincts*.

5. Many animals can learn new behaviors. When a dog avoids a skunk, it is using ___learned behavior.___ _____

6. Scientists have found that animals learn new behaviors in the following three ways: ___through conditioning, trial and error, and reasoning.___ _____

7. The Russian scientist Ivan Pavlov discovered conditioning. In his experiment, he found that he could make dogs' mouths water by ___ringing a bell that they associated with food.___ _____

8. Scientists realized that when chimps piled up boxes to reach bananas, they were learning a new behavior through reasoning. The chimps were using past experiences ___to solve a new problem.___ _____

Animal Communication

1. Social animals, such as buffalo, ants, and wolves, live _together in groups._

2. Animals who live in groups do many things together. The term *social behavior* describes how animals _respond to group living._

3. Animals' different positions in their group are called the *social order*. Respect for the social order makes animals _behave better to each other._

4. In some animal groups, such as insect colonies, a social behavior called *division of work* means that all the members _have their own jobs to do._

5. When animals communicate, they send signals to _change the behavior of other animals._

   Some ways they communicate are _growing, showing teeth, and leaving a "scent trail"._

6. Humans communicate by using language. Researchers have asked whether other animals _communicate in the same way._

The Scientist at Work

7. In 1960, Jane Goodall was amazed to see a chimpanzee _poke a grass stick into a termite hole to fish for termites._

   After years of observations, Goodall concluded that chimpanzees _make and use simple tools._

8. In Goodall's study of chimpanzees, she used the three scientific methods of _observation, repetition, and inferring from evidence._

9. Goodall found that chimpanzees communicate by using different _sounds, facial expressions, and body movements._

10. Goodall was able to understand the general meaning of many chimpanzee sounds when she _noticed how other chimpanzees responded to the sounds._

Keeping in Touch

Fill in each of the blanks with the word from the box that best completes each sentence.

inferior	vital	dominance	subordinate
superior	hierarchy	status	elaborate

Scientists studying animal behavior have learned that it is essential, even _____vital_____, to separate puppies no later than seven weeks after birth. If they are left in the litter any longer, a pecking order, or _____hierarchy_____, will be established. The largest, strongest puppies will actively display their _____dominance_____ and bully the other pups. The smaller, less aggressive puppies will avoid the larger puppies. These larger puppies act as if they are better than the others and as if their size makes them _____superior_____. Once the puppies have established their _____status_____, they will maintain that position for life, and it will be reflected in their personality no matter how their size changes. The large puppies will always keep their aggressive personality. They will not be _____subordinate_____ to any other dog, no matter how big or strong that other dog may be. Expensive, complicated, and _____elaborate_____ training programs will fail to change their behavior. And what of the smaller, bullied puppies? Even if they grow bigger than the dogs that once bullied them, they will always feel _____inferior_____ and will cower at the other dogs all of their lives. This may at first seem unfair of nature, but in the wild, the hierarchy of the pack may be a necessary component of unity and survival.

Keeping in Touch

Before Reading As you begin the selection, review the questions you would like answered about wolves.

Read pages 502–510. As you read, note how the authors of "Keeping in Touch" categorize information to organize their ideas about the social structure and communication within a wolf pack. Then come back to this page and write about those categories below.

The Dominance Hierarchy Within a Wolf Pack

(Sample answers)

Category	Status	Characteristics
Alpha male and alpha female	Leaders of the pack	oldest members; most experienced hunters and protectors of the pack; decision makers for the pack
Young adult wolves	Subordinate to alpha pair	have special roles under parents' leadership; may dominate other young adults because of superior size, strength, or personality
Juveniles and pups	Subordinate to all adults	no permanent positions within hierarchy; constantly competing for top position within age group

What are the categories of communication among wolves? sounds, smells, movements, and body positions

Choose two categories of wolf communication and give examples of those that fall within those categories. (1) *body positions:* dominance indicated by high position of tail, ears that stand up, and fur that fluffs out; subordinate wolves show respect through active submission and use passive submission as a kind of apology for disrespectful behavior; (2) *sounds:* group howling to show closeness; lone howling when wolf is separated from pack

After Reading Can you answer the *Thinking and Discussing* questions on page 511? If not, reread the selection, using the Stop and Think Strategy as needed.

Keeping in Touch

Write the answer to each question below. Look back at the selection if you need help.

(Sample answers)

1. Why do wolves always travel in groups, or packs? <u>because the pack, usually a family group, is the basic unit of wolf social life</u>

2. What are the pack leaders called? <u>the alpha male and the alpha female</u>

3. Besides the leaders, what wolves live in the pack? <u>the leaders' offspring — young adult wolves, juveniles, and pups</u>

4. Why are some wolves called *dominant* wolves? <u>They boss their age group through superior physical strength or more aggressive personalities.</u>

5. How do wolves communicate with each other? <u>by sounds, smells, movements, and body positions</u>

6. What is most of the communication among pack members about? <u>rank and position in the pack</u>

7. How do the alpha male and female show their importance by the position of a body part? <u>They carry their tails up high.</u>

8. How does a wolf change the position of its body to show friendly feelings and respect for the alpha wolf? <u>It keeps its body low, with fur and ears flat.</u>

9. Why does a wolf lie down and show its belly to a more dominant wolf? <u>to show harmlessness</u>

10. What message does a wolf communicate by bowing and wagging its tail? <u>"Let's play!"</u>

11. How does a wolf send a message to the pack from a distance? <u>by howling</u>

Never Cry Wolf

Fill in each of the blanks in the following journal entry with the word from the box that best completes each sentence.

amiable	improbable	incredulous	obscure	ritual
converse	encountered	coincidence	intercept	skepticism

I must admit that I miss the comforts of home, but out here in this land of frozen lakes, it is easy to forget all other worlds. But even a few short weeks ago, I would have said that it was highly __improbable__ for me to be backpacking — winter camping — in this isolated place. I can still remember the unbelieving, __incredulous__ look on my best friend's face when I first announced my plans. And my mother didn't bother to hide her __skepticism__ when she said I'd last twenty minutes.

But finally, they gave me their support, and we said goodbye in a friendly, __amiable__ way. This has not been the first time I have __encountered__ a lack of belief in my ability to do something that seemed challenging or out of character.

I am trekking over some __obscure__ terrain. It is so remote and unknown, it cannot be found on any map. It is no __coincidence__ that my group leader suggested we each bring a compass.

As soon as the sun begins to lower in the western sky, we must begin our search for the night's campsite. Our late afternoon activity is so important to our survival that it has become a __ritual__. We each have specific duties: One group prepares the site; one gathers firewood; one sets up the tent. Anything __converse__ to this would mean danger. If the dark and wind __intercept__ or stop the progress of our actions, we will be left vulnerable to the elements. But when we are successful, we have only to sit around enjoying the fire.

Never Cry Wolf

Before Reading   As you begin the selection, recall what you want to learn about wolves in "Never Cry Wolf."

Read pages 512–518.   As you read, pay careful attention to details in order to help you identify main ideas. Then return to this page to complete the boxes below.   (Sample answers)

Main idea: Ootek can in fact understand wolf communication, or perhaps the events occurred coincidentally.

Supporting details: Ootek claims to interpret George's cry that reveals the existence and location of caribou. Mike packs for a hunting trip in pursuit of caribou. Mike returns having caught venison where Ootek said the caribou would be. (pages 514–515)

Main idea: The author is very skeptical about wolf language and humans' ability to understand it. (pages 514–515)

Supporting details: The author calls Ootek's story "improbable" and a "fantastic yarn." The author is surprised that Mike would go out on a hunt based on Ootek's story. The author is convinced that the incident is coincidence and begins to question Ootek's and Mike's judgment.

Main idea: Ootek may indeed understand wolf communication.

Supporting details: Ootek claims to have heard George indicate that he would not return until midday. The wolves return at 12:17. Ootek is asleep during the wolves' return. (page 516)

Main idea: The author may be more open to the idea that Ootek understands wolf communication. (page 518)

Supporting details: George cocks his ears to the north. Ootek becomes excited and heads off to the northwest. The wolves prepare for their evening hunt, and, instead of going north or northwest as they usually do, they go east. Ootek returns with three Eskimos.

After Reading   Can you answer the *Thinking and Discussing* questions on page 519? If not, reread the selection, using the Stop and Think Strategy as needed.

Never Cry Wolf

Complete the outline below. Look back at the story if you need help.

(Sample answers)

Setting <u>1946, near a wolf den in northern Canada</u>

Characters <u>The narrator, Farley Mowat; Mike, a native trapper; Ootek, an Eskimo</u>

_____

_____

Problem   Mowat doesn't believe that <u>wolves can talk or that humans can</u>
<u>understand them.</u>

_____

Events

1.   Ootek tells Mowat that the wolves' howls mean <u>caribou are coming.</u>

Mike goes hunting and finds caribou where <u>Ootek said they would be.</u>

_____

2.   Ootek claims that George howled a message to Angeline, telling her
that <u>he wouldn't be home until midday.</u>

In fact, George returned at 12:17.

3.   Ootek tries to tell Mowat that the wolves' howls mean <u>"Eskimos come."</u>

_____

Ootek leaves and later returns with <u>three Eskimo friends.</u>

_____

Conclusion   Ootek seems to understand the wolves' communication.
Mowat may be ready to believe that <u>wolves can communicate and that some</u>
<u>humans can understand them.</u>

_____

Dolphins: Our Friends from the Sea

In each group of words below, draw a line through the word that does not belong in the group. Then briefly tell how the other three words belong together.

mimic ~~outcry~~ imitate copy

All words except *outcry* mean "to copy (someone or something)."

_____

potential promise capability ~~friendliness~~

All words except *friendliness* imply that future success is possible.

_____

contest ~~agree~~ dispute challenge

All words except *agree* mean "to argue about or challenge (something)."

_____

murky cloudy ~~transparent~~ muddy

All words except *transparent* describe water or some other liquid that

cannot be seen through.

counter oppose debate ~~locate~~

All words except *locate* mean "to speak or argue against."

_____

frolic ~~endure~~ romp play

All words except *endure* mean "to enjoy oneself."

_____

speculates guesses ~~accepts~~ predicts

All words except *accepts* mean "thinks about and makes a prediction about what

might happen."

Do you think dolphins "speak" to each other? On a separate sheet of paper, express your opinion about dolphin communication. Use as many of the vocabulary words as you can.

Dolphins: Our Friends from the Sea

Write the answer to each question below. Look back at the selection if you need help.

(Sample answers)

A Mysterious Attraction

1. What reason does Dr. John Lilly give for dolphins' attraction to humans? (page 522) Dolphins want to communicate with us.

Dolphin Language

2. According to Jacques Cousteau, why do dolphins make a variety of sounds? (page 523) to communicate and to locate themselves by echoes

3. What do the Caldwells think dolphins use sounds for? (page 524) for special reasons, while swimming or playing, and to echolocate themselves

Dolphins and Human Language

4. What does Dr. Lilly believe about the dolphin brain? (page 524) It is as large and complex as a human brain and shows that dolphins can learn as much as humans.

5. According to the Caldwells, why do dolphins have such large brains? (page 527) Dolphins' large brains are useful for echolocation.

6. What technique does researcher Robert McNally say that Dr. Lilly used to train dolphins to speak? (page 528) brainwashing

Do Dolphins Understand?

7. What do the Caldwells say about whether dolphins communicate intelligently? (page 529) Dolphins learn to make certain sounds only because they respond to sound cues.

8. What did Jarvis Bastian's experiment show about Buzz's and Doris's responses? (pages 529–530) They were responding to cues, not communicating.

9. What does Dr. Lilly believe about dolphin communication? (page 530) They communicate in a way we don't understand.

Koko

Answer each of questions 1–9 with one of the words from the box.

abstractly	ambidextrous	edible
excels	gesture	impervious
incorporated	indisputable	novelty

1. What does a policeman use to direct cars to turn left? _gesture_____

2. Which word refers to foods it is safe to eat? _edible_____

3. Which word is the opposite of *fails*? _excels_____

4. What word describes a person who is comfortable using either a right or a left hand? _ambidextrous_____

5. To understand an idea or a concept you cannot touch or see, how must you think? _abstractly_____

6. Which word is the opposite of the expression *old hat*? _novelty_____

7. Which word means "combined into a unified whole"? _incorporated_____

8. Which word describes an argument based on facts and eyewitness accounts? _indisputable_____

9. Which word describes someone who is unaware and not paying any attention? _impervious_____

Now answer the following questions. Make sure your answer shows that you understand the italicized vocabulary word.

(Answers will vary.)

10. Why would it be convenient or useful to be *ambidextrous*? _____
_____
_____
_____

11. Are all *edible* plants delicious? Explain. _____
_____
_____
_____
_____

12. If someone is *impervious* to your requests to use the telephone, what do you do? _____

_____

13. If someone tells you that a rule you dislike is *indisputable*, how will you feel? _____

_____

14. How could an exercise program be *incorporated* into your busy schedule?

_____

_____

_____

Write a paragraph describing what factors or efforts make it possible for someone to *excel* in one of the following areas: sports, music, art, writing.

_____

_____

_____

_____

_____

_____

_____

_____

_____

_____

_____

_____

_____

_____

_____

_____

_____

_____

_____

_____

Koko

Before Reading   Review the questions you would like answered by "Koko" and keep them in mind as you read the selection.

Read pages 532–538.   As you read, consider why it may be useful to identify the most important points in an informational article. Then come back to this page to complete a summary of "Koko" below.

(Sample answers)

Penny Patterson is fascinated by the work of the Gardners, who <u>taught a chimp sign language</u>. She teaches a gorilla named Koko <u>sign language and English</u> by <u>molding and talking to the gorilla</u>. Patterson gives Koko IQ tests in order to determine <u>Koko's intelligence, which is just below the human average</u>.

She determines the extent of Koko's vocabulary by <u>recording the signs that the gorilla uses at least fifteen days in a month</u>.

Koko has surpassed people's expectations by <u>starting conversations on her own; demonstrating the ability to think abstractly; showing a grasp of time, colors, and numbers; and creating new words already in her vocabulary</u>.

Koko can now communicate using two languages — <u>sign language and computer-assisted English</u>.

Patterson's work has raised questions such as <u>Do gorillas have their own language? Can thought exist without language?</u>

After Reading   Can you answer the *Thinking and Discussing* questions on page 539? If not, reread the selection, using the Stop and Think Strategy as needed.

Koko

Write "True" or "False" after each sentence below. Then explain your answer on the line. **(Sample answers)**

1. Penny Patterson was the first person to teach language to an ape. **False.** **Patterson became interested in the topic after hearing psychologists Allen and Beatrice Gardner describe their work with Washoe.**

2. Patterson taught Koko only Ameslan (American Sign Language), which was used by the Gardners to teach Washoe, a chimpanzee. **False. Patterson also taught Koko English.**

3. Patterson taught Koko by "molding" Koko's hands into the different signs. **True. The Gardners developed this method to teach Washoe to sign.**

4. Koko can do some things better than human children can. **True. Koko can swing from a bar and climb a tree better than any child her age.**

5. Patterson measures Koko's vocabulary according to a system used by the Gardners. **True. Koko has to use a sign at least fifteen days in a month for it to qualify as learned vocabulary.**

6. Koko's measured vocabulary at seven years was 375 words. After that she stopped learning new words. **False. She is still learning new signs.**

7. When a visitor arrived in a flowered skirt, Koko proved she knew the difference between the picture of a flower and the actual flower. **True. She has two signs for *flower*, and she uses the signs appropriately.**

8. Koko has made new words by stringing together signs she already knows. **True. A ring is a "finger-bracelet," and a zebra is a "white tiger."**

9. Koko can communicate in sign language but not in spoken words. **False. Koko uses a machine to express spoken words.**

10. Since Koko has learned to use language, she behaves less like a gorilla and more like a human. **False. Like any gorilla, Koko play-bites, likes to sleep in a nest, and isn't bothered by pain.**

11. Scientists agree that because Patterson taught Koko to use language, she also taught Koko to think. **False. Scientists disagree about whether thinking can take place without formal language.**

Noting Details to Identify Main Ideas and Make Inferences

The following selection tells about insect communication. Read the selection, and then answer the questions.

Insect Communication

Insects, like other animals, have three major ways of communicating.

Many insects communicate by producing sounds. A male tarantula hammers a love song at the female with his four front legs. To sing to their mates, crickets may rub their wings together or rub their legs against their wings. Flies also express themselves with their wings, making a loud, angry buzz when they are trapped, for example. Bees buzz angrily at an intruder near their hive. Velvet ants (a type of wasp) squeak warnings to other velvet ants. Grasshoppers, too, warn others of their species — by rubbing their legs together in flight. Grasshoppers also make clicking sounds to frighten their enemies.

A second type of insect communication is the use of visual signals — colors, dances, or strange movements. Because of special light organs in their bodies, male fireflies flash patterns of light to attract female fireflies. In response, the females flash back their own distinctive light patterns. Some insects, such as wasps, have warning colors that alert their enemies to stay away. Some insects' coloring looks like that of dangerous species; harmless flies and moths may resemble wasps or bees. Bees dance to direct other bees to newly discovered food; the motions of the dancing bee tell the hive members what direction to fly in and how far to travel. A male jumping spider attracts females with his bright colors. Then the male waves his arms and dances until a female joins him.

A third type of insect communication is based on smell and taste. Some smells are alarms, or warnings to stay away. The stinkbug, for instance, produces a vile-smelling, vile-tasting spray that warns insect-eating birds and animals of an unpleasant meal. Aphids may secrete an odor that warns other aphids to retreat from danger. Some insect smells are used to attract mates. For instance, certain female spiders weave silk threads with an odor that attracts males of their species. Other insects leave scent trails that direct other insects to food or to the nest. Honeybees, for example, mark the entrance to their nest as well as sources of food to aid other members of their hive.

1. What are the three methods of communication discussed in this article? Incorporate your answer into a statement that gives the main idea of the whole selection. <u>**Insects communicate through sounds, through visual signals, and through smell and taste.**</u>

2. What main idea is stated in the second paragraph? "Many insects communicate by producing sounds."

   What other statement could sum up the information in that paragraph? (Sample answer) Insects use sounds to communicate a variety of messages.

3. What can you infer to be the method that many insects use to produce sounds? Insects may create sounds by rubbing body parts together, rather than by using their voices.

4. What main idea is stated in the third paragraph? "A second type of insect communication is the use of visual signals — colors, dances, or strange movements."

   What other statement could sum up the information in that paragraph? (Sample answer) Insects use visual signals to attract mates, give warnings, and direct other group members to food.

5. What are some inferences you can make using details about insects' visual signals? Insects may have a good sense of sight; animals who eat insects must somehow know to avoid those with warning colors; male and female insects of some species live apart and must first find each other in order to mate; insects have developed varied ways to use visual signals.

6. What main idea is stated in the fourth paragraph? What details support that main idea? "A third type of insect communication is based on smell and taste." Supporting details: Stinkbugs and aphids use odors as warnings; insects may use odors to attract mates; insects may leave scent trails or marks to direct others to food or to the nest.

7. What details from the selection support this inference: Insects are able to communicate with other species. Bees buzz angrily at an intruder; grasshoppers use clicking sounds to frighten enemies; warning colors tell enemies to stay away; stinkbugs warn enemies with a strong odor.

Cause-Effect in Science Writing

The following selection tells about one kind of animal communication. Read the selection, and then answer the questions.

Chemical Communication

Many animals — from dogs, skunks, and rabbits to turtles, fish, and silkworms — communicate by producing chemical "messages." These messages, known as **pheromones** (FARE-uh-mones), are detected by other animals of the same species as odors or tastes. They vary from a mammal's scent markings on a tree to a female silkworm moth's chemical mating call, which attracts male moths from up to a mile away, although humans cannot smell it. These animal messages convey a range of meaning: "Come to me." . . . "Stay away." . . . "This is my territory." . . . "Here's home." . . . "This is the queen bee." . . . "It's too crowded here." . . . "I'm tough."

Research into chemical signals started at the beginning of the twentieth century with the study of moth and butterfly messages. Over fifty years passed before two German biologists isolated and identified the first pheromone — **bombykol** (BOM-bih-kol). To extract a gram of bombykol, they used more than one-half million silkworm moths. Since then, scientists have discovered about a thousand pheromones.

Pheromones are produced in small organs called **glands.** The location of these glands varies widely from species to species. The black-tailed deer, for example, has a gland below each eye. The silkworm moth's is on the tip of its abdomen. A rabbit's scent gland is located on its chin, a lemur's on its chest, a mouse's on its feet, and a cat's around its mouth and forehead. When a cat rubs its head against you, it leaves behind a chemical message that other cats may receive. Some animals have specialized structures for these glands, such as the **scent brushes** of certain butterflies. Different animals release their pheromone chemicals in different ways — by spraying, rubbing, radiating, depositing, or dusting. They do so in response to certain stimuli in their environment, such as danger or the presence of a member of the opposite sex.

The study of pheromones may have practical applications in the future. Bees are essential for pollenating flowers and plants. Someday, farmers may be able to use certain pheromones to draw bees to their crops. Other pheromones may be used in traps to catch insect pests. Or they may be used to confuse male insects during the mating season.

1. What main purpose do pheromones serve? <u>They chemically communicate</u> <u>messages to other members of the same species.</u>

2. Why does a female silkworm moth give off pheromones? <u>to attract a mate</u>

3. What other things can pheromone messages help an animal to do? <u>An animal</u> <u>can find its home, recognize its leader, or skirt an area that belongs to its enemy.</u>

4. Perhaps you have seen an animal sniffing at a tree or rock. What is a likely cause of that behavior? <u>The animal is sniffing for a chemical message that</u> <u>another animal has left behind. The first animal may have announced that it passed</u> <u>this way or that the tree or rock is in its territory.</u>

5. What causes animals to release pheromones? <u>stimuli in the environment, such</u> <u>as danger or a member of the opposite sex</u>

6. What may be some future effects of the scientific study of pheromones? <u>practical applications such as attracting bees to pollenate crops and</u> <u>catching or controlling insect pests</u>

7. The last paragraph ends with a statement about using pheromones "to confuse male insects during the mating season." What effect would that use have? <u>The confused male insects would not be able to mate. As a</u> <u>result, the insects would not reproduce, and their population would go down.</u>

BOOK 8

The Pushcart War, Part I

campaign	theory	provoking	inevitable
menace	commended	zeal	sound

Think about the meaning of the words in the box. Write each word beside its definition.

__menace__   Someone or something that threatens harm

__zeal__   A strong, eager feeling, as in working for a cause

__campaign__   A series of military operations that achieves a specific purpose in a certain area

__sound__   Sensible and correct

__provoking__   Arousing; bringing on

__inevitable__   Not capable of being avoided or prevented

__theory__   A statement or statements designed to explain things observed

__commended__   Mentioned with approval; praised

Now use the words in the box to complete the analogies below.

act : play :: __campaign__ : war

problem : solution :: __menace__ : helper

strength : exercises :: __theory__ : experiments

scolded : blame :: __commended__ : compliment

flawed : wrong :: __sound__ : accurate

Do you experience zeal when you think about a cause that you care about? On a separate sheet of paper, write a description of what you might do to bring about a change in something you care strongly about. Use as many words from the box as you can.

The Pushcart War, Part I

Setting   New York City, March 15, 1986

The author immediately establishes the time and place of the Pushcart War. She vividly describes New York traffic, since the War takes place in the streets. Describe an incident from the first part of the novel that could only happen in the streets of a city like New York. Include three descriptive words from the opening chapters. (Answers will vary.)

_____

_____

Complete each incomplete sentence below. Look back at the selection if you need help. After some incomplete sentences, the page numbers of the answers are given.   **(Sample answers)**

Characters and Plot

The Pushcart War starts when Mack the trucker flattens Morris the Florist's pushcart, although Morris feels he has a right to the space (page 552). Kindly Frank the Flower helps Morris buy a new cart from Maxie Hammerman, the Pushcart King.

Maxie knows all about New York pushcarts and gives peddlers good business advice. People started to see that trucks, not pushcarts, caused the crowded streets. Even movie star Wenda Gambling said publicly that there were too many trucks (page 567).

Truck owners Louie Livergreen, Big Moe, and the Tiger plotted against the pushcarts. Louie hates pushcarts because his father was a pushcart peddler. The truckers smashed pushcarts and blamed the accidents on the pushcarts (page 574).

Theme

Professor Cumberly and Jean Merrill both state that there won't be peace until people understand how wars start.

The Daffodil Massacre shows that wars can start when people want the same space (page 552).

The Pushcart War, Part II

Imagine that you are a reporter assigned to cover all community activities. Recently a local seventh grade class discovered a polluted stream near its school. For the next issue of the paper, you are going to interview the students about what they found and what they are doing. Write the answers the students give you. In each answer, use a word from the box that has the same meaning as the italicized words in the question.

casualties	contaminated	convictions
inconvenience	morale	proposed

1. What have you found out about what caused the stream to be *polluted*? (Answers will vary but should contain the word *contaminated*.)

2. How did you all feel about finding fish and other *dead, wounded, and injured inhabitants* of the stream floating in the stream? (Answers will vary but should contain the word *casualties*.)

3. How did finding all that pollution so close to your school affect the *state of your spirits*? (Answers will vary but should contain the word *morale*.)

4. What are some of the possible solutions you have *put forward* for the town to consider? (Answers will vary but should contain the word *proposed*.)

5. Which one of the solutions do you think will be best even if it causes *trouble or difficulty*? (Answers will vary but should contain the word *inconvenience*.)

6. What do you think has helped you develop *strong opinions and beliefs* about clean air and water? (Answers will vary but should contain the word *convictions*.)

The Pushcart War, Part II

Setting

Describe the battle headquarters at Maxie's shop. Show that the

peddlers and Maxie are well-organized and prepared to fight back.

(Answers will vary. Selection words may include *red* and *gold pea-pins,*

well-organized, huge street maps and *very neat.*)

_____

_____

Complete each incomplete sentence below. Look back at the
selection if you need help. After the last incomplete sentence, the
page number of the answer is given.

(Sample answers)

Characters and Plot

The peddlers meet at Maxie's to raise money for Morris the Florist's
new cart. Maxie shows leadership and brains by
explaining why the truckers are behind the accidents.

When Old Anna urges the peddlers to fight back, they name her
General Anna and prepare the Pea Shooter Campaign.

Peaceful Mr. Jerusalem finds he likes to fight back when
Little Miltie insults him. General Anna shows

she is brave and resourceful when she kills fourteen tires by hand.

Frank the Flower is arrested and heroically shoulders the blame for
shooting 18,991 tires.

Theme

Mr. Jerusalem's change of heart shows that sometimes it's necessary
to fight to protect one's rights as a human being (page 588).

The Pushcart War, Part III

Complete each definition below by writing the correct vocabulary word.

averting	confiscated	conspiracy
discriminated	improvised	jubilant
phase	repealed	unnerved

_____phase_____ A distinct stage of development

_____unnerved_____ Caused to lose courage and confidence

_____jubilant_____ Full of joy; rejoicing

_____confiscated_____ Seized in order to be withheld, redistributed, or destroyed

Now create a scene that might have been left out of *The Pushcart War.* Choose some *Pushcart* characters to use in the scene. Use as many of the vocabulary words as you can.

(Answers will vary.)

_____

_____

_____

_____

_____

_____

_____

_____

_____

_____

_____

_____

_____

_____

The Pushcart War, Part III

Setting

Describe the time and place of the peddlers' conference after the raid
on Maxie's. Show how the big-city setting of the conference adds to
the feeling of General Anna's and the peddlers' determination. (Answers will vary.)

_____

_____

Complete each incomplete sentence below. Look back at the
selection if you need help. After some incomplete sentences, the
page numbers of the answers are given.

(Sample answers)

Characters and Plot

In the Pea Shooter Campaign — Phase II, children use pea shooters
to kill tires. The Tacks Tax and the Pea Blockade lead to
the raid on Maxie's shop. General Anna shows her
leadership after Maxie's arrest when she keeps the peddlers from
surrendering. Thinking quickly, Maxie is released when he
tells the Police Commissioner his map of New York is a business
chart (page 620).

At a meeting of the Three, Louie Livergreen says peddlers don't
have any fighting spirit and will give up when Maxie is kidnapped.
Maxie learns about the kidnap plot from Miriam Portlette's notes
(page 629). Maxie invites the Three to a poker game with the Police
Commissioner and wins $60,000 (page 634).

Theme

When people try to control public feelings about an unfair situation,
such as the Tacks Tax and the Pea Blockade, the public
becomes determined to fight back.

The Pushcart War, Part IV

Use the words in the box to complete the letter below. Then reread the letter with a friend.

amnesty	unamimous	manifesto
compromise	begrudge	brilliant
revoked		

To Our Leader,

We are writing in secret to let you know about the most recent developments in our part of the campaign to move our political cause forward successfully. First, we have asked the government to pardon and grant _____amnesty_____ to our workers who were arrested last week. As you know, they were caught planting flowers in a part of the park that the government is planning to turn into a parking garage. We are happy to report that officials are prepared to _____compromise_____ with us as long as we promise to plant no more flowers in construction areas. We are prepared to present the government with a _____manifesto_____ issued by the founders of this city. It promises citizens that their environment will remain unspoiled. The founders were _____unanimous_____ in their support of preserving the environment for citizens.

Second, we do have licenses to protest in front of the capitol and to hold public rallies in the park, but the government met late last night to see if the licenses can be _____revoked_____. Apparently some officials, worried about our ability to excite citizens about our cause, _____begrudge_____ us our popularity with the public. But the public support is stronger than ever. We think this part of the campaign to stop construction in the park has been _____brilliant_____. In other words, your advice has been excellent. What do you think we should do next?

Yours Truly,

Workers for the Cause

The Pushcart War, Part IV

Setting

Describe the setting of the Peace March. Include details that appeal to the different senses. (Answers will vary.) _____

_____

_____

Complete each incomplete sentence below. Look back at the selection if you need help. After some incomplete sentences, the page numbers of the answers are given.

Characters and Plot   (Sample answers)

Maxie tells Eddie Moroney it is better to have enemies that

_____ you can see and that fear you _____ (page 635). He says

he's putting the _____ $60,000 into a War Chest for the Pushcart War _____.

During a truce, the truckers wreck more pushcarts.

To press for a peaceful settlement, Mr. Jerusalem organizes

_____ a Peace March _____. But Mack the trucker drives into the Peace

Army _____ to crush Morris the Florist _____ (page 645).

Mayor Cudd suspends the pushcart peddlers' licenses because he

says _____ they broke the truce _____ (page 649).

When Marvin Seeley's photo of the Daffodil Massacre

_____ appears in the newspaper _____, readers' angry letters

force the Big Three to hold _____ a Peace Conference with Maxie

_____ Hammerman to work out an agreement _____ (page 663).

Conditions for peace include the following: _____ Mammoth Moving _____

will pay for Mack's damaging the Peace Army; Mack's license will be

revoked for a year; there will be smaller and fewer trucks, on the

basis of Frank the Flower's Flower Formula; Frank the Flower has

amnesty _____ (pages 663–668).

Theme

The letter-writing campaign shows that each person can

play a part in making great changes _____. The success of the

Flower Formula says that the best solutions are often _____ the simplest _____.

Understanding How Details Convey the Elements of a Novel

Read the following excerpt from the opening of *The Adventures of Tom Sawyer* by Mark Twain. Then answer the questions.

"**T**om!"

No answer.

"Tom!"

No answer.

"What's wrong with that boy, I wonder? You TOM!"

No answer.

The old lady pulled her spectacles down and looked over them about the room; then she put them up and looked out under them. She seldom or never looked through them for so small a thing as a boy; they were her state pair, the pride of her heart, and were built for "style," not service — she could have seen through a pair of stove lids just as well. She looked perplexed for a moment, and then said, not fiercely, but still loud enough for the furniture to hear:

"Well, I lay if I get hold of you I'll — "

She did not finish, for by this time she was bending down and punching under the bed with the broom, and so she needed breath to punctuate the punches with. She resurrected nothing but the cat.

"I never did see the beat of that boy!"

She went to the open door and stood in it and looked out among the tomato vines and "jimpson" weeds that constituted the garden. No Tom. So she lifted up her voice at an angle calculated for distance and shouted:

"Y-o-u-u Tom!"

There was a slight noise behind her and she turned just in time to seize a small boy by the slack of his roundabout and arrest his flight.

"There! I might 'a' thought of that closet. What you been doing in there?"

"Nothing."

"Nothing! Look at your hands. And look at your mouth. What *is* that truck?"

"I don't know, aunt."

"Well, I know. It's jam — that's what it is. Forty times I've said if you didn't let that jam alone I'd skin you. Hand me that switch."

The switch hovered in the air — the peril was desperate —

"My! Look behind you, aunt!"

The old lady whirled round, and snatched her skirts out of danger. The lad fled, on the instant, scrambled up the high board fence, and disappeared over it.

His aunt Polly stood surprised a moment, and then broke into a gentle laugh.

1. What details about the setting can you find in this selection?
   The setting appears to be a small house. Outside the house is a yard, and beyond

   that, a fence. There is a closet in the house, in which Tom hides.

2. Who are the main characters introduced in this scene? **Tom Sawyer and his**
   Aunt Polly

3. Twain does not describe either character directly. Indirectly, however,
   he creates physical impressions of them. What do you know about
   them from the opening selection? What details give these
   impressions? **We know that Aunt Polly is old and somewhat slow-moving; in**
   contrast, Tom is young, small, and quick. In the beginning, Aunt Polly makes many

   small movements that extend over time. When she is looking for Tom, she breathes

   heavily while punching under the bed with the broom. In contrast, Tom is gone in an

   instant — the moment Aunt Polly turns her back.

4. What do you learn about Aunt Polly from the details about her
   glasses? Explain your answer.
   She is older now but still slightly vain. For the sake of style, she wears glasses

   that serve no practical function.

5. What do you learn about Tom from the details about his hiding
   place?
   He's mischievous and sly; hiding in the closet, he'd been eating jam.

6. In the end, what does Polly's gentle laugh reveal about her character?
   She's warm-hearted and loving toward Tom, despite her wish to punish him.

7. The details help develop the themes that are introduced in this
   opening scene. What are those themes?
   adulthood versus childhood; the "crimes" of childhood

The excerpt from The Adventures of Tom Sawyer *continues on
page 129.*

Understanding Satire

This excerpt from *The Adventures of Tom Sawyer* began on page 127. It continues below. Read the next excerpt; then answer the questions that follow.

While Tom was eating his supper, and stealing sugar as opportunity offered, Aunt Polly asked him questions that were full of guile, and very deep — for she wanted to trap him into damaging revealments. Like many other simple-hearted souls, it was her pet vanity to believe she was endowed with a talent for dark and mysterious diplomacy, and she loved to contemplate her most transparent devices as marvels of low cunning. She said:

"Tom, it was middling warm in school, warn't it?"

"Yes'm."

"Didn't you want to go in a-swimming, Tom?"

A bit of a scare shot through Tom — a touch of uncomfortable suspicion. He searched Aunt Polly's face, but it told him nothing. So he said:

"No'm — well, not very much."

The old lady reached out her hand and felt Tom's shirt, and said:

"But you ain't too warm now, though." And it flattered her to reflect that she had discovered that the shirt was dry without anybody knowing that that was what she had in her mind. But in spite of her, Tom knew where the wind lay, now. So he forestalled what might be the next move:

"Some of us pumped on our head — mine's damp yet. See?"

Aunt Polly was vexed to think she had overlooked that bit of circumstantial evidence, and missed a trick. Then she had a new inspiration:

"Tom, you didn't have to undo your shirt collar where I sewed it, to pump on your head, did you? Unbutton your jacket?"

The trouble vanished out of Tom's face. He opened his jacket. His shirt collar was securely sewed.

"Bother! Well, go 'long with you. I'd made sure you'd played hooky and been a-swimming. But I forgive ye, Tom. I reckon you're a kind of a singed cat, as the saying is — better'n you look. This time."

She was half sorry her sagacity had miscarried, and half glad that Tom had stumbled into obedient conduct for once.

But Sidney said:

"Well, now, if I didn't think you sewed his collar with white thread, but it's black."

"Why, I did sew it with white! Tom!"

But Tom did not wait for the rest. As he went out at the door he said:

"Siddy, I'll lick you for that."

1. What is satire? Why does an author use satire? <u>Satire is writing that mocks</u>
   <u>certain behaviors and attitudes. Authors often use satire to express their opinions</u>
   <u>about people or situations.</u>

2. In the opening of this passage, the author gently pokes fun at Aunt
   Polly. How does he do this? <u>Twain shows that Polly regards herself as clever and</u>
   <u>cunning, when in reality she is constantly outsmarted by Tom, a young boy.</u>

3. What message does Twain seem to be trying to convey through this
   use of satire? <u>He is conveying the idea that Aunt Polly is not nearly as cunning as</u>
   <u>she thinks she is. He may also be implying that people often think they are</u>
   <u>something they are not — that people can be vain, and too proud, or conceited, and</u>
   <u>so on.</u>

4. How does the fact that Tom has been sneaking sugar behind Aunt
   Polly's back during dinner contribute to this satire? <u>The fact that Tom can sneak</u>
   <u>sugar so easily underscores the idea that Aunt Polly is not so cunning as she</u>
   <u>supposes herself to be.</u>

5. What trait of human nature was the author satirizing in the
   statement that Aunt Polly "was half sorry her sagacity had
   miscarried, and half glad that Tom had stumbled into obedient
   conduct for once"? <u>People do not like to be proved wrong about anything — even</u>
   <u>if being proved wrong is in their best interests.</u>

6. What happens at the end of the scene to show that the gentle
   mocking of Aunt Polly was deserved? <u>Tom slips quickly out the door. He had been</u>
   <u>swimming when he was supposed to be in school, after all.</u>

Dictionary/Glossary

Read the two word entries, one from a dictionary and the other from a glossary. Use the information to answer the questions below.

Dictionary Entry

face (fās) *noun* **1.** The front part of the head from the forehead to the chin. **2.** An expression on the face: *You have a happy* face. **3.** A twisting of the muscles of the face; grimace: *Don't make* faces. **4.** The surface presented to view; the front: *The* face *of my watch is broken.*
verb **1.** To have the face or front toward: *Turn around and* face *the class.* **2.** To deal with boldly, firmly, or bravely: *I just can't* face *the problem today.*

Glossary Entry

face (fās) *n.* The surface presented to view; the front: *the north* face *of a building.*

---

1. What do dictionaries and glossaries both contain? **words and their definitions**

2. How is the dictionary entry different from the glossary entry? **It contains multiple definitions for the word, including its meaning as a different part of speech.**

3. What is generally the purpose of a glossary? **to define words for the reader as they are used in context *in the book in which they appear***

4. Write a sentence using a definition of *face* from the dictionary and the definition of *face* from the glossary.
   (Answers will vary.)

Parts of a Book

This sample table of contents is from a book about the Civil War.

Write the title of the section or sections from the table of contents where you would look to find answers to these questions.

1. What caused the Civil War? <u>**Differences Divide the North and South, Slavery,**</u>
<u>**Economic Growth, Political Differences**</u>

2. Which were the major battles during the war? <u>**Major Battles, Gettysburg:**</u>
<u>**A Turning Point**</u>

3. Why did General Lee surrender? <u>**Lee's Surrender**</u>

The index below would be at the back of the book on the Civil War. Use it to answer the questions that follow.

Index

4. If you were writing about slavery, what index entry would you use? <u>**slavery**</u>
<u>**issue**</u>

5. Which section can guide you to information on women in the war — the table of contents or the index? <u>**the index**</u>

Adjusting Reading Rate

Read the passage below. Adjust your reading rate to be an effective reader. Then answer the questions below.

"What a fine biscuit I have!" thought the dog as he trotted across the narrow bridge. He held the biscuit tightly in his mouth and raised his head and tail proudly.

Halfway across, the dog glanced over the side of the bridge at the water below. He saw another dog looking up at him, also holding a biscuit. Snarling, he lunged to grab the other dog's biscuit. In doing so, he dropped his own into the water.

The dog barked angrily at his shattered reflection. Then he walked home, wondering how that clever dog had stolen his biscuit.

Is this a narrative or an expository passage? __narrative__

How do you know? __It tells a story and contains language similar to that of speech.__

Would you read this passage quickly or slowly? Explain. __Since this passage was easy to comprehend and my purpose in reading was enjoyment rather than mastery of facts, I would read it quickly.__

Read the passage below, and adjust your reading rate accordingly. Then answer the questions that follow.

A light source smaller than the object it shines on produces a dark shadow, called an *umbra*. This is because the object stops all the light falling on it. A light source larger than the object it shines on produces an umbra as well as a lighter shadow, called a *penumbra*, because some of the light shines past the object into the shadow and lightens the outer part of it.

What kind of passage is this? __expository__

How can you tell? __It does not tell a story. It was written to explain something.__

If your purpose in reading this passage was to do research for a report, would you read it slowly or quickly? Explain. __I would read this passage slowly to make sure I understood it, and to remember the technical details accurately.__

Gather a stack of all the books, magazines, and other materials you are currently using in school or reading on your own. Decide what reading rate you should use with each one and why. Use those adjusted reading rates when you read the material.

Skimming and Scanning

Skim the following passage to get a rough idea of its content. Then answer the questions that follow.

How Is Sound Created?
Sound is created when an object vibrates, causing the air, water, or other medium around it to vibrate also. These vibrations, or *sound waves*, travel outward, getting weaker and weaker as they move away from the object that caused them.

How Does Sound Travel?
Sound waves need a substance such as water, air, or the ground to travel through. This substance is called the *sound medium.* The speed at which sound travels is affected by the density and temperature of the sound medium through which it is traveling.

1. What is the main topic of this article? _sound_____

2. What are the two subtopics? _How sound is created and how it travels_____
   _____

3. Were the following ideas mentioned? Write *yes* or *no* after each.

   the human ear _no_____ sound in outer space _no_____

   sound waves _yes_____ vibrations _yes_____

   Read each question below, and scan the partial index to answer the questions.

   sound, 13, 148–151
         breaking of sound barrier, 241
         pitch, 150
   sound recording
         compact disk, 222
         digital, 309, 311
         Dolby sound, 223–224
         phonograph, 177–179
   sound waves, 148–151
         intensity, 150
         measuring, 151

4. From scanning the index, do you think that this book would be helpful if you were writing a report on methods of sound recording?
   Explain. _Yes. Several methods are listed._____

5. On the use of sound effects? _No. This topic is not mentioned._____

6. On hearing aids? _No. This topic is not mentioned._____

7. On high and low sounds? _Yes. The topic *pitch* would have information on this_
   topic._____

Using the Library Catalog

Use these cards from a library's catalog to answer the questions below.

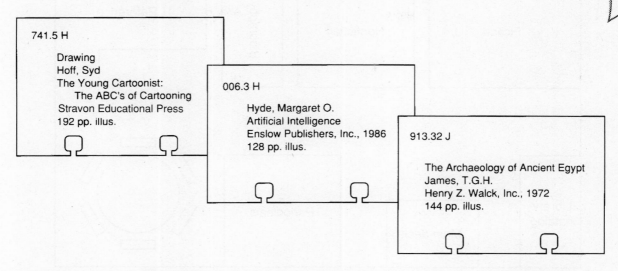

741.5 H

Drawing
Hoff, Syd
The Young Cartoonist:
    The ABC's of Cartooning
Stravon Educational Press
192 pp. illus.

006.3 H

Hyde, Margaret O.
Artificial Intelligence
Enslow Publishers, Inc., 1986
128 pp. illus.

913.32 J

The Archaeology of Ancient Egypt
James, T.G.H.
Henry Z. Walck, Inc., 1972
144 pp. illus.

1. Which of the above cards is a *title card* — top, middle, or bottom? **bottom**

2. Who is the author of the book on the *author card*? **Margaret O. Hyde**

3. What is the call number of the book *Artificial Intelligence*? **006.3 H**

Read each question. After each, write down what kind of card — *author, title,* or *subject* — would best help you find the answer.

4. Did Beverly Cleary write any books of nonfiction? **author**

5. Were *Sixteen* and *Seventeen* written by the same author? **title**

6. What books does the library have on careers in mathematics? **subject**

7. Who wrote *The Way Things Work*? **title**

8. Has Ronald Reagan ever written a book? **author**

9. Does this library have any books on making musical instruments? **subject**

10. How many books does the library have by Agatha Christie? **author**

11. Has Madeleine L'Engle written any nonfiction books for young people? **author**

12. Is *Green and Growing* a book on gardening? **title**

Choose two fiction and two nonfiction books from those you have at home or in your classroom. Using 3" x 5" index cards or pieces of paper, make out a subject, a title, and an author card for each one. In place of a call number, write "fiction," "nonfiction," or "biography" in the top left corner of each card.

Using the Library

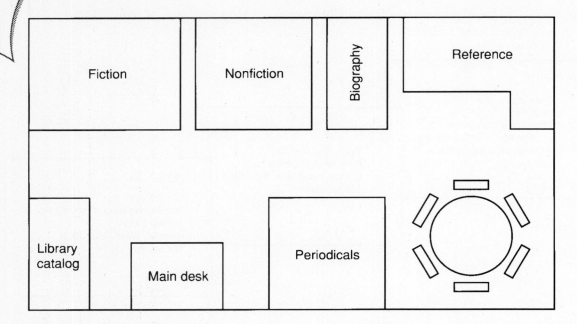

Fiction

Nonfiction

Biography

Reference

Library catalog

Main desk

Periodicals

Refer to the labeled diagram of a library. Then, after each question below, write the name of the section of the library where you would go to answer the question.

1. What magazine articles on space flight have been written recently? <u>**periodicals**</u>

2. What are the titles of some nonfiction books on the Vietnam War? <u>**library catalog**</u>

3. Does the book *The Adventures of Tom Sawyer* by Mark Twain contain much dialogue? <u>**fiction**</u>

4. What are the current national and world records held in the long jump, pole vault, and 100-yard dash? <u>**reference**</u>

5. How did world-renowned violinist Yehudi Menuhin become interested in music? <u>**biography**</u>

6. Did the *New York Times* publish any articles on the destruction of the Berlin Wall? <u>**periodicals**</u>

7. Which of the books on wind surfing has the most informative photographs? <u>**library catalog, then nonfiction**</u>

8. What are the basic facts of John F. Kennedy's life? <u>**reference or biography**</u>

Special Reference Sources

Read the description of each reference source below.

A *dictionary* gives meanings and pronunciations of words. Some dictionaries include word histories.

An *encyclopedia* contains articles on many subjects. It is a good place to find basic information about a subject.

A *thesaurus* contains synonyms. It will help you find a word that is close in meaning to a word you know. Some thesauruses also give antonyms.

An *almanac* contains lists of facts and statistics. It is a good resource for current information.

An *atlas* is a book of maps.

Write the best reference source to use for answering these questions. Then tell why you chose that reference source.

1. Are there any mountainous regions in Georgia? An atlas would be best, because maps show mountains.

2. What words mean almost the same as *interesting*? A thesaurus would be best, because it contains synonyms.

3. Does *brougham* rhyme with *home*? A dictionary would be best, because it has pronunciations of words.

4. Which singer had the biggest hit single last year? An almanac would be best, because it contains current information.

5. How is a telescope made? An encyclopedia would be best, because it contains basic information on many subjects.

Visit the reference section of a local or school library. Look at several examples of each kind of reference source. Which dictionary, thesaurus, atlas, almanac, and encyclopedia do you find most interesting? Why?

(Answers will vary.)

_____

_____

_____

_____

Encyclopedia

Answer the questions below. You may want to refer to an encyclopedia as you answer the questions.

1. What kind of book is an encyclopedia? **reference book**

2. How are the articles in an encyclopedia arranged? **alphabetically from A to Z**

3. How do you locate information in an encyclopedia? **by using the volume letters, guide words, and encyclopedia index**

Use this section of an encyclopedia index to complete the chart and answer the questions.

Motion Picture
Animation A:511
Camera C:80
Copyright (Works Protected) Ci:1047
Disney, Walt D:237

Motocross [race]
Bicycle Racing B:294–295 with picture; picture on B294
Motorcycle (Motorcycling as a Sport) M:879

Mott, Lucretia Coffin [American Social Reformer] M:880
Abolition Movement (In the United States) A:13
Woman suffrage (Beginnings of the movement) W:382

	Topic	Volume	Page(s)
1.	Disneyland's founder	D	237
2.	motocross bike racing	B	294–295
3.	voting rights for women	W	382
4.	cartoon movies	A	511
5.	antislavery organization	A	13

1. In which volume and on what page might you look if you wanted to learn about movie cameras? **Volume C, page 80**

2. If Volume M did not have all the information you needed about Lucretia Mott, in which other volumes might you look? **Volumes A and W**

3. In which volumes might you look if you wanted to compare bicycle racing and motorcycle racing? **Volumes B and M**

Newspaper

Suppose that your local newspaper ran this article. Read it carefully. Then answer the questions below.

Glenn Valley Loses Power
by Carl Thomas, Staff Reporter

Glenn Valley, Nov. 20 — It was a black night for the residents of Glenn Valley, who lost electric power last night. From 6:00 P.M. yesterday until shortly after 5:00 this morning, the town of Glenn Valley and part of Coppertown experienced total power failure.

a. What is the headline of this article? "Glenn Valley Loses Power"

b. What information does the by-line tell you? The article was written by Carl Thomas, a staff reporter.

c. Where and when was the article written? Glenn Valley, on November 20

d. Answer the following questions from the lead.

Who? residents of Glenn Valley

When? last night

What? lost electric power

Where? Glenn Valley and part of Coppertown

Read the headlines below and write the name of the section in which each belongs — Classified, Editorial, Entertainment, News, or Sports.

a. "For Sale: Used Books" Classified

b. "Science Class Gets Pet Boa" News

c. "New Teen Movie a Real Dud" Entertainment

d. "Panthers Squash Pandas in Double Overtime" Sports

e. "One Seventh-Grader's Opinion" Editorial

Think of something that has happened lately in the news or in your school. Write a lead paragraph about the event that answers the questions *who, what, when,* and *where.* Include a headline, by-line, and dateline if you wish. (Answers will vary.)

Maps

Study the simplified political map of New Mexico below. Use the information from the map to answer the following questions.

1. What is the state capital of New Mexico? **Santa Fe** How can you tell? **It is marked with a star.**

2. Which city has a major airport? **Albuquerque** How can you tell? **The symbol for a major airport is next to Albuquerque.**

3. Which U.S. states border New Mexico? **Texas, Arizona, Oklahoma, Colorado (accept Utah)**

4. Is Route 25 an interstate highway or a U.S. highway? **interstate** How can you tell? **The highway number is written in a shield with a band at the top.**

5. What symbol is used to indicate national boundaries? **a solid line together with a dashed line**

6. About how many miles is it from Roswell to Carlsbad? **75**

7. What county seat is closest to the state of Oklahoma? **Clayton**

8. If you drive west from Socorro on Route 60, what town will you come to eventually? **Pie Town**

9. Which cities or towns are located along Route 54? **Alamogordo, Carrizozo, Corona, Santa Rosa, and Tucumcari**

10. Using only the highways indicated on the map, what would be the shortest route between Gallup and Wagon Mound? **Starting at Gallup, go east on Route 40 to Albuquerque; then take Route 25 northeast to Wagon Mound.**

11. Would a jumbo jet be able to land at Santa Fe? **no** Why or why not? **There is no major airport at Santa Fe.**

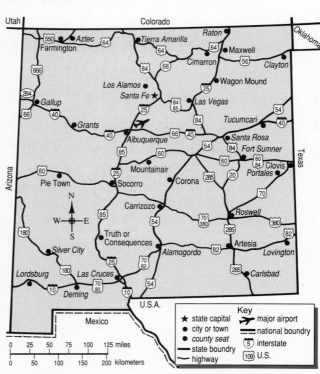

Graphic Aids: Charts, Diagrams, Graphs, Tables

Use the graph below to answer the following questions.

1. What kind of graph is shown? <u>bar</u> Why are bar graphs well suited to comparing information? <u>(Answers will vary.)</u>

2. What school lunch is the least favorite of the seventh grade students? <u>chef's salad</u> How many students chose it? <u>two</u>

3. What two lunches were chosen by the same number of students? <u>spaghetti and fried chicken</u>

4. List the three favorite lunches in order, starting with the most favorite.
<u>taco, pizza, hamburger</u>

Use the chart below to answer the following questions.

5. How many people work under the editor-in-chief of the newsletter? <u>ten</u>

6. Who is the poster artists' direct supervisor? <u>posters head</u>

7. Which editor has only one staff reporter? <u>litter editor</u>

8. Does the secretary supervise any other workers? If so, whom? <u>yes, two typists</u>

On a separate sheet of graph paper, make a scale drawing of the floor plan of your bedroom or of some other room in your house or apartment. Include size and placement of windows, doors, furniture, and rugs.

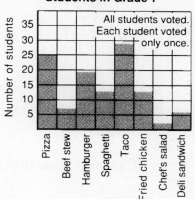

Favorite School Lunch of Students in Grade 7

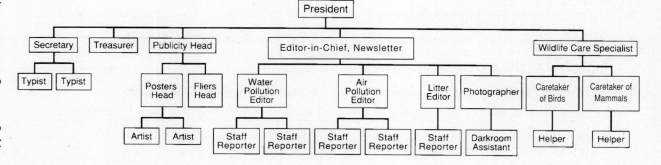

Ecology Center Staff

Graphic Aids: Making a Time Line

Read the following passage about the life of Walt Disney. Use the space below to create a time line of his accomplishments.

Walt Disney was born in 1901, but his best-known creation, Mickey Mouse, did not appear until 1928. Walt Disney and his brother, Roy, launched their own company, Disney Productions, in 1919. The first full-length color cartoon ever made, *Snow White and the Seven Dwarfs*, was released in 1937, to be followed by others, including *Fantasia* (1940), *Dumbo* (1941), and *Cinderella* (1950). In addition to his work in films, Disney invented the theme park in 1955 with the opening of Disneyland. At the time of his death, on December 15, 1966, he was planning Walt Disney World and EPCOT Center in Florida. Both opened after his death — Walt Disney World in 1971 and EPCOT Center in 1982.

Walt Disney

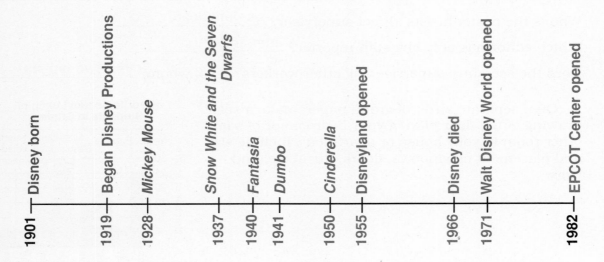

Use your time line to answer these questions.

1. How old was Disney when he started Disney Productions? __eighteen__
2. In what year did Mickey Mouse first appear? __1928__
3. Which came first, the opening of Disneyland amusement park or the opening of the movie *Cinderella*? __Cinderella__
4. What two milestones in Disney's career actually happened after his death? __the opening of Walt Disney World and the opening of EPCOT Center__

Gathering Opinions

Read the paragraph, and then answer the questions.

You are in charge of hiring a band for the next dance. You aren't sure whether a rap band or a rock band would appeal to more seventh grade students. You decide to take a poll to find out.

(Sample answers)

1. What question might you use to gather opinions? <u>Which would you prefer to hear</u> <u>at our next dance, a rap band or a rock band?</u>

2. What are two methods you could use to gather opinions? <u>Provide students with</u> <u>ballots on which to indicate their opinions, or question students orally.</u>

3. How could you record students' answers? <u>Make a table with two columns headed</u> <u>*rap music* and *rock music.* In each column, keep a tally of students' replies.</u>

4. How could you be sure that you have gathered a reliable sample? <u>Poll a number</u> <u>of students from different homerooms and with different interests.</u>

The questions below were taken from polls conducted by students. After each, tell whether or not you feel the question is appropriate and well worded, and why.

(Sample answers)

5. What kinds of candy do you like the most? <u>No. It will produce too many answers</u> <u>to record easily.</u>

6. What was your opinion of the movie *Alien*? Check one.
   ☐ liked it a lot ☐ it was O.K. ☐ disliked it <u>Yes. It gives people a chance to</u> <u>state their opinions without producing too many answers.</u>

7. You didn't like that horrible stew we had for lunch, did you?
   <u>No. The questioner's opinion may influence the way others respond.</u>

8. What was your **one** main reason for attending the game yesterday?
   Check one. ☐ I like sports. ☐ One of my family members is on the
   team. ☐ I wanted to be with friends. ☐ I didn't have anything else
   to do. ☐ Other (specify) <u>Yes. It limits the number of possible answers while</u> <u>allowing some freedom.</u>

9. How old are you? <u>No. It produces too many answers.</u>

10. What is your age in years? Check one. ☐ 5–10 ☐ 11–13 ☐ 14–16 ☐ 17–19
    ☐ 20 or over <u>Yes. It limits the number of possible answers.</u>

Evaluating Information

Read the advertisement below. Then answer the questions.

(A) Flyrite Sneakers are by far the most comfortable sneakers available. (B) Athletes who try Flyrites will see a great improvement in their game. (C) As the owner of Flyrite Sports Company, I know firsthand that no other sneakers are better for your feet. (D) Flyrites are sold at all Finney, Douglas, and Sole shoe stores. (E) For two weeks only, they will be priced at only $49.95.

1. Is sentence A a statement of fact or opinion? __opinion__

   How do you know? __It cannot be proved.__

2. Which statement shows author bias? __sentence C__ Why do you think the writer is biased? __because he or she owns the company__

3. How can you tell that sentence B is an assumption? __The writer makes this statement as if it were a proven fact.__

4. Which sentences are factual? __sentences D and E__ How could you prove these facts? __by calling or visiting the stores__

Now evaluate this speech.

(A) I am challenging our student-body president because I feel he lacks an interest in school sports. (B) As last year's president, my opponent did not participate in school sports. (C) Perhaps his lack of interest is the reason he did nothing to stop some sports from being cut. (D) His lack of effort will keep hundreds of students from winning sports scholarships. (E) My opponent is a loser and will bring you defeat, but I am a winner and will bring you victory.

5. Which sentence states a fact? __sentence B; it can be proved__

6. Which two sentences express opinions? __sentences A and C__

7. Which sentence is an assumption? __sentence D__

8. How can you tell from sentence E that the author is biased? __The speaker uses emotional words: *loser, defeat, winner, victory.*__

Outlining

Read the following article about poisonous snakes. As you read, notice the topics, subtopics, and details that you would use to outline the article.

Poisonous Snakes

There are basically two different kinds of poisonous snakes. Some snakes are capable of inflicting a fatal wound; others are not. Poisonous snakes with fangs at the back of the mouth are not usually dangerous. Because of the placement of their fangs on the upper jaw, it is difficult for them to sink the fangs into humans or animals quickly.

The other group of poisonous snakes is dangerous and deadly. These snakes have fangs in the front of the mouth. The fangs, which may be shed and replaced several times each year, are needle-sharp. In some snakes, the fangs fold back and are protected by the roof of the mouth. Of the two kinds of poisonous snakes, most are front-fanged. So if you ever find yourself facing an angry snake, make a hasty retreat! A few snakes to watch out for are copperheads, rattlesnakes, and water moccasins.

Now outline the facts contained in the article so you can see how they are related.

Poisonous Snakes

I. Not dangerous

    A. Fangs at back of mouth

        1. Fangs on upper jaw

        2. Difficult to sink in quickly

II. Very dangerous

    A. Fangs at front of mouth

        1. May be shed and replaced

        2. Needle-sharp

        3. Some fold back — protected by roof of mouth

    B. Most snakes front-fanged

    C. Kinds: copperheads, rattlesnakes, water moccasins

Choose another article about animals from your science textbook, the encyclopedia, or another source. After reading the article, outline the information on a sheet of paper in order to better understand it. Remember to start with the topic of each paragraph and then look for subtopics.

Taking Notes

As you read the article below, take notes on the important details you want to remember about sleep.

Understanding Sleep

People spend about one third of their lives sleeping. No one knows exactly why we sleep, but it seems to be necessary for the health of both the mind and the body.

The amount of sleep someone needs depends on several things, including age. Most newborn babies sleep nearly all day. Four-year-olds average from ten to fourteen hours of sleep a day, and ten-year-olds average from nine to twelve hours. Most adults sleep seven to eight hours every night.

People who go without sleep for more than thirty-six hours become irritable. Someone who has stayed awake for more than three days will begin to hallucinate — to see and hear things that are not there.

_____

_____

_____

_____

_____

_____

_____

_____

_____

_____

_____

What heading did you use? **(Answers will vary.)** _____

_____

What subheadings did you use? **(Answers wil vary.)** _____

_____

Which subheading had the most details under it? **(Answers will vary.)** _____

_____

_____

Categorizing Information

Read the list of activities that you might find in an article on physical fitness. Then write each activity in the best category.

long-distance running	soccer
basketball	dancing
roller-skating	baseball
volleyball	Ping-Pong

Team sports
- basketball
- volleyball
- soccer
- baseball

Individual sports
- long-distance running
- roller-skating
- dancing
- Ping-Pong

Now categorize each activity according to whether it uses a ball or does not use a ball.

Uses a ball
- basketball
- volleyball
- soccer
- baseball
- Ping-Pong

Does not use a ball
- long-distance running
- roller-skating
- dancing

Which of these activities are offered in your gym class and which are not? Write them in the categories below.

Offered in gym class
(Answers will vary.)

Not offered in gym class

What other ways might you categorize these activities? (Answers will vary.)

Outlining and Summarizing from Notes

On a separate sheet of paper, take notes about the different kinds of exercises discussed in the following article on working out.

Working Out

Health experts recommend a thirty-minute workout of continuous exercise each week. Every workout should include three types of exercises: flexibility, endurance, and strengthening exercises.

Flexibility exercises include stretching, bending, and twisting movements. They should be done before and after each workout to reduce the risk of injury and soreness.

Endurance exercises, also called aerobic exercises, range from running to swimming. These activities are beneficial for the heart, circulation, and breathing.

Strengthening exercises include pull-ups, pushups, and sit-ups. They strengthen the arms and shoulders, as well as other muscular parts of the body.

Organize your notes by completing the outline below.

Working Out

I.   (Answers will vary.) _____

    A. _____

II. _____

    A. _____

    B. _____

    C. _____

III. _____

    A. _____

        1. _____

        2. _____

    B. _____

IV. _____

    A. _____

    B. _____

Provide a quick reminder as to what this article is about by writing a summary from your notes on a separate piece of paper.

Summarizing Stories and Informational Text Graphically

A. Read each question below. Decide whether the information asked for could best be summarized graphically by a diagram, chart, map, table, graph (circle, line, or bar), or time line.

1. What are the parts of a grand piano? <u>diagram</u>

2. How many pairs of sneakers did Suarez's Footwear sell each day for the week of May 15? <u>bar graph</u>

3. What is the organization of the administration of your school? <u>chart</u>

4. What is the best route to follow between City Hall and the Village Green? <u>map</u>

5. What dates mark important developments in the history of the computer? <u>time line</u>

B. Read the paragraph below. Then choose the best way to summarize the information graphically. Draw what the final product might look like and insert the information from the paragraph.

Lawrence Book Nook sells paperback books. The store sold 300 books in January, 200 in February, 350 in March, 400 in April and in May, 600 in June, 800 in July, 850 in August, 600 in September, 750 in October, 500 in November, and 1000 in December.

(Students may choose either a table or a line graph. A possible response follows.)

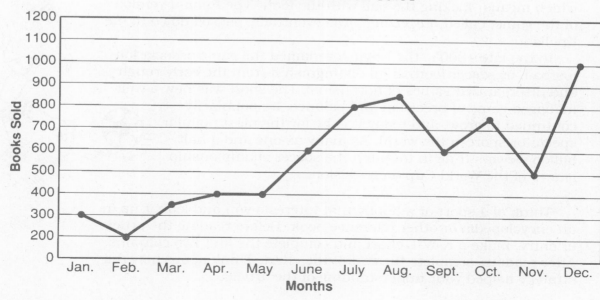

Lawrence Book Nook Sales

K-W-L

Use the K-W-L Strategy as you read the informational text below.

Before you begin reading, look to see what the topic of the text is. Then complete the first two columns of the K-W-L chart. Next, read the passage on the history of soccer at the bottom of the page. After you have read the passage, complete the third column of the K-W-L chart.

(Answers will vary.)

What I know	What I want to find out	What did I learn? What do I still want to know?

The History of Soccer

Soccer has been around in one form or another for thousands of years; it is the oldest sport in history. Many believe soccer was first played by the Chinese 2500 years ago. They called it *tsu chu*, which means "kicking the ball with the foot." The Roman version of the game, called *harpastum*, was eventually passed down to the English.

In the late 1800's, the English renamed the game association football, or soccer football, to distinguish it from the early rough and disorganized games of *harpastum*. The sport was now a well-managed game of precision and balance. Its popularity continued to grow, and today it is by far the most popular spectator sport in the world. As many as one and a half billion viewers tune in to watch the soccer championship games of the World Cup on television.

Think of a sport or a hobby that interests you and look it up in an encyclopedia or other reference book. Before reading the article or entry, make a K-W-L chart and complete the first two columns. After reading, complete the rest of the chart. Think about how the strategy helped your understanding of the article.

SQP3R

Use the SQP3R Strategy as you read the textbook selection. Following these steps will help you:

1. **S**urvey   Make a check by each thing you survey.

2. **Q**uestion   Turn the headings into questions and write them on a separate sheet of paper.

3. **P**redict   Predict the answers to your questions. Write your predictions on a separate sheet of paper.

4. **R**ead   Think about your predictions as you read.

5. **R**ecite   Use what you have read to recite the answers to your questions. Write the answers on a separate sheet of paper.

6. **R**eview   Review each heading. Recall what question you turned it into and the answer to that question.

Roller Skating

The inventor of roller skates did not see great success. In fact, he was nearly killed demonstrating his new idea.

The Invention of Roller Skates

In 1760, Joseph Merlin invented the first pair of roller skates. He fitted small metal spools to wooden strips, and then fastened the wooden pieces to his feet with straps. After inventing the skates, Merlin demonstrated his new invention. The roller skates moved along well enough, but he crashed because he couldn't stop. No one thought very much of his dangerous new invention.

Plimpton Perfects the Skate

A hundred years later, safer roller skates were developed. In 1863, James Plimpton made a skate similar to the roller skates used today. It consisted of four wheels attached to a metal plate. The wheels were positioned so that skaters could control the skates simply by leaning in one direction or another.

The First Roller-skating Rink

Plimpton knew that people would need a place to skate, so he built the first skating rink. It was a fancy rink in Newport, Rhode Island. To ensure its success, Plimpton had a grand opening. The rink was such a huge success that he built another rink in New York City. Eventually, he built many rinks around the country. Roller-skating soon grew to be very popular.

Think of a period of history that interests you and locate an article on it in your history textbook. Read the article using the SQP3R Strategy for reading. Follow the steps outlined above and write your responses on a separate sheet of paper.

Organizing Study Time

Joshua and Jason had a midyear test scheduled for Friday, December 14. Read each student's notebook and compare how the boys organized their study time. Then answer the questions that follow.

Joshua

Sunday	Monday	Tuesday	Wednesday	Thursday	Friday	Saturday
2	3 *Play basketball*	4	5	6 *Study ½ hour – math*	7	8
9	10	11	12 *Study math while watching Raiders*	13 *Study LATE!!! Test Tomorrow*	14 *Test math*	15

Jason

Sunday	Monday	Tuesday	Wednesday	Thursday	Friday	Saturday
2	3 *★GOAL★ Get a B on math mid-year*	4 *Study 4:00 – 5:00*	5 *Study 4:00 – 5:00*	6 *Math quiz Study 4:00 – 5:00*	7 *Study 4:00 – 5:00*	8
9	10 *Study 4:00 - 5:00*	11 *Study 4:00 - 5:00*	12 *Prep for math – Study 3:00 – 5:00*	13 *Study 3:00 - 4:00*	14 *Midyear test – math 11:00*	15

1. Did both students set a goal? Explain. **Jason set a goal of getting a B on his math test. Joshua did not set a goal.**

2. Which student's study plan probably worked better? Give two reasons why. **(Answers will vary, but should state that Jason's plan worked better because he set a goal, studied at the same time every day, and prepared for the test.)**

3. Why wouldn't Joshua have gotten a lot of studying done the night the Raiders game was on television? **Television is distracting while studying.**

4. Was Joshua's plan for studying late the night before the test a good idea? Explain. **It was probably not a good idea, because he may have been tired for the test and performed poorly.**

5. Why is studying at the same time every day a good idea? **You become organized, and studying becomes a habit.**

6. How could using SQP3R help Joshua and Jason while studying math? **Study techniques such as SQP3R help students organize and remember what they read.**

Test-Taking Strategies

Use what you have learned about tests to complete the following items.

Essay Tests

1. An essay test is one that requires you to <u>write an essay or a number of paragraphs on what you know about certain aspects of a subject.</u>

2. To prepare for an essay test, you should <u>study broad topics and main ideas, along with supporting details and examples.</u>

3. When writing answers to an essay test, you should remember to <u>begin each paragraph with a main idea and add details that support it.</u>

Objective Tests

4. Objective tests include many items that ask for <u>specific information.</u>

5. Item formats for objective tests may include <u>true-false questions, short-answer questions, multiple-choice questions, and matching items.</u>

6. When preparing for an objective test, you should be sure to study <u>names, dates, and events.</u>

7. When taking an objective test, you should <u>read directions and items carefully, eliminate answers you know are wrong, and look for clue words that help you eliminate other answers.</u>

Which type of test do you prefer? Explain your answer.

(Answers will vary.)

_____

_____

_____

_____

_____

_____

Language and Usage Lessons

Overview

Language and Usage Lessons have been provided in the *Student Resource Book* as an optional resource for teachers who wish to integrate these skills into their reading/language arts curriculum. A Capitalization, Punctuation, and Usage Guide has also been provided as a useful handbook for students' own reference.

The Language and Usage Lessons provide opportunities for direct instruction in key language areas. Instruction, modeling, guided practice, and independent practice are provided for each skill. Students using *Houghton Mifflin Reading: The Literature Experience* will have a rich variety of reading, writing, listening, and speaking projects and activities; this section provides a useful support for those language arts areas.

The Language and Usage Lessons are organized into the following five major sections: The Sentence, Nouns, Verbs, Pronouns, and Phrases and Clauses.

Format of the Lessons

Each lesson is two pages in length. The first page provides instruction and guided practice. The second page provides a skill reminder and independent practice. Instruction, written to the student, can be used as a basis for a teacher-led discussion. Suggestions for modeling each lesson can be found on pages 217–220 of the *Student Resource Book, Teacher's Annotated Edition.* Guided practice begins with an example and gives students an opportunity to practice the skill with the guidance and support of the teacher. Directions for the independent practice are clearly written and easy to follow. An example is provided to reinforce both the directions and the skill.

How to Use the Lessons

The teacher's goals, style of teaching, and classroom organization will guide the use of this section. Because the lessons are grouped into skill categories and in many cases build sequentially, it is best to use them in the order presented. Some ideas for incorporating the lessons into your teaching plan follow.

1. You might decide to incorporate the five language and usage skill categories into the eight themes in the student anthology. For example, you might introduce the Capitalization, Punctuation, and Usage Guide during Theme 1, AT THE EDGE, and encourage students to familiarize themselves with its contents so they can use it independently. You might then teach the lessons in the section The Sentence with Theme 2, the lessons in Nouns with Theme 3, the first four lessons in Verbs with Theme 4 and the last four with Theme 5, the lessons in Pronouns with Theme 6, and the first three lessons in Phrases and Clauses with Theme 7 and the last three with Theme 8.

2. You might choose to use this section as a resource to supplement your own or a published instructional program in language, mechanics, and usage.

The flexibility of this section permits it to be used in a variety of ways. You, as a teacher, will know best how to use it.

Capitalization, Punctuation, and Usage Guide

This guide is a helpful handbook for student reference throughout the year. It can also be used for instruction. It includes the following sections, with rules and examples provided for each section: Abbreviations, Bibliography, Titles, Quotations, Capitalization, Punctuation, Problem Words, Adjective and Adverb Usage, Negatives, Pronoun Usage, and Verb Usage.

This guide will be a valuable resource to students in their writing. Throughout the year you might want to remind students of the existence of this resource and to refer them to it whenever they indicate in their speech or writing a need for this support.

The most common conjunctions are *and, but,* and *or.* These are called **coordinating conjunctions.** They connect words or groups of words that are equal in importance and perform the same function in the sentence.

Each coordinating conjunction shows a different relationship between the ideas it connects.

Coordinating Conjunction	Relationship
and	joining or addition of similar ideas
but	contrast or difference between ideas
or	choice between ideas

Rice **and** fish are traditional foods of Japan.
Beef was unknown there a century ago **but** is now common.
The Japanese eat seaweed dry, **or** they use it in soup.

Some conjunctions are used in pairs. These pairs are called **correlative conjunctions.** Correlative conjunctions make an even stronger connection between ideas than a coordinating conjunction does.

Neither oils **nor** fats are used in Japanese cooking.

Common Correlative Conjunctions	
both . . . and	neither . . . nor
either . . . or	whether . . . or

GUIDED PRACTICE

You will need to guide students through the Guided Practice activity, providing support as necessary.

A. Which coordinating conjunction best fits each sentence?

Example: Americans _____ people of other countries eat many of the same foods. *and*

1. Americans may produce the food in the United States, _____ they may import it from other countries. **or**

2. Some foreign foods _____ recipes are not popular here. **and**

3. The Spanish sometimes eat fried eels, _____ most Americans do not enjoy that dish. **but**

B. Identify the correlative conjunctions in each sentence.

Example: Both hamburgers and pizza are considered American foods.
Both   and

4. Neither hamburgers nor pizza was first eaten in America.   **Neither . . . nor**
5. Both German hamburgers and Italian pizza have become part of
   the American diet.   **Both . . . and**
6. Many other "American" foods either were brought to America by
   Europeans or came from other continents.   **either . . . or**

REMINDER

- **Coordinating conjunctions** join words or groups of words.

- **Correlative conjunctions** are used in pairs to join words or groups of
  words.

Coordinating Conjunctions	Correlative Conjunctions
and but or	both . . . and either . . . or
	whether . . . or neither . . . nor

  Spanish explorers found pineapples in South America **and** took some
  home.
  Both Florida **and** Hawaii are states with pineapple fields.

INDEPENDENT PRACTICE

Write the coordinating and correlative conjunctions in these
sentences.

Example: Both pineapples and coconuts grow in Hawaii.   **Both . . . and**

1. Europeans did not know about pineapples until
   1493, but South Americans enjoyed them hundreds
   of years earlier.   **but**

2. King Louis XIV tasted one of the first pineapples in
   France, but he did not enjoy it.   **but**

3. He bit into the unpeeled fruit and cut his lip.   **and**

4. The King was angry and ordered people not to
   grow the fruit.   **and**

5. Both Africa and Australia have pineapple fields.   **Both . . . and**

6. These continents grow both tomatoes and olives
   as well.   **both . . . and**

7. Neither tomatoes nor olives are usually thought of
   as fruits.   **Neither . . . nor**

You can create complex sentences by combining simple sentences.

SIMPLE: Divers discover shipwrecks. Scientists study them.
COMPOUND: Divers discover shipwrecks, and scientists study them.
COMPLEX: When divers discover shipwrecks, scientists study them.

You can use the conjunction *and* to combine almost any related sentences. *And* simply means addition. It does not tell very much about how the sentences are related.

The ship sank, **and** the divers descended.

By using subordinating conjunctions rather than *and*, you can often make the meaning much clearer. Notice how the meaning changes with different subordinating conjunctions.

As soon as the ship sank, the divers descended.
Where the ship sank, the divers descended.

Use a comma after a subordinate clause at the beginning of a sentence. In most cases, do not use a comma before a subordinate clause at the end of a sentence.

When the wreck was explored, Spanish coins were found.
Spanish coins were found **when the wreck was explored.**

GUIDED PRACTICE

Combine each pair of simple sentences into a complex sentence, using the conjunction in parentheses. Use commas wherever they belong.

Example: Shipwrecks are time capsules. People study them.
(because)
Because shipwrecks are time capsules, people study them.

1. A sunken ship can tell us something about the past. It is studied carefully. (if)   If it is studied carefully, a . . .
2. There are thousands of shipwrecks in American waters. Many have not been found. (although)
3. No one discovers it. A ship can sit at the bottom of the sea for centuries. (if)   If no one discovers it, a . . .
4. Some wrecks should not be disturbed. Time and money are available for a complete study. (until)
5. Wrecks can be lost. People wait too long. (if)
Wrecks can be lost if . . .

Although there are thousands of shipwrecks in American waters, many . . .

Until time and money are available for a complete study, some . . .

REMINDER

- You can combine simple sentences to form complex sentences. A subordinating conjunction tells how the sentences are related.
- Use a comma after a subordinate clause at the beginning of a sentence.

Simple: The hippopotamus is large. The elephant is larger.
Complex: **Although** the hippopotamus is large, the elephant is larger.

INDEPENDENT PRACTICE

Combine each pair of simple sentences into a complex sentence, using the conjunction in parentheses. Use commas where they are needed.

Example: Elephants will charge. They are scared. **(if)**   (Sample answers)
Elephants will charge if they are scared.

1. Elephants slide on their bellies. They go down steep hills. **(when)**
Elephants slide on their bellies when they go down steep hills.

2. An elephant herd walks quietly. It travels single file. **(as)**
An elephant herd walks quietly as it travels single file.

3. Elephants are large. They are easy to tame. **(although)**
Although elephants are large, they are easy to tame.

4. They are easily tamed. You often see elephants in circuses. **(because)**
Because they are easily tamed, you often see elephants in circuses.

5. The elephant eats. It finds grasses, bark, or twigs. **(wherever)**
The elephant eats wherever it finds grasses, bark, or twigs.

6. Elephants do not eat meat. They must eat a lot of grass. **(because)**
Because elephants do not eat meat, they must eat a lot of grass.

7. An elephant grows permanent tusks. It is two years old. **(when)**
An elephant grows permanent tusks when it is two years old.

8. Elephants can run fast. They sense danger. **(if)**
Elephants can run fast if they sense danger.

A word that names a person, a place, a thing, or an idea is called a **noun.**

Diane read a **book** about **inventors** in **Japan.**

Concrete and Abstract Nouns

A noun that names something that can be seen, smelled, heard, tasted, or touched is called a **concrete noun.** An **abstract noun** names an idea, a quality, or a feeling.

CONCRETE NOUNS: Uncle Joe, village, vegetables
ABSTRACT NOUNS: belief, beauty, disappointment

GUIDED PRACTICE

Identify the nouns in these sentences. Which nouns are concrete? Which are abstract?

          concrete   abstract
1. Some early inventors had little education.

        concrete   abstract
2. These pioneers worked alone on their dreams.

      concrete   concrete   abstract
3. Modern businesses hire people with creative abilities.

      concrete   concrete   concrete
4. These designers develop new products, such as safer toys.

    concrete   concrete   concrete
5. Scientists work with engineers on amazing gadgets.

Common and Proper Nouns

A **common noun** refers to any person, place, thing, or idea. Do not capitalize common nouns.

A **proper noun** identifies a particular person, place, thing, or idea. Proper nouns are always capitalized. If a proper noun contains two or more words, each important word in the noun is capitalized.

COMMON NOUNS	PROPER NOUNS
city	Houston, Quebec, Tel Aviv
ocean	Atlantic Ocean, Indian Ocean
people	North American, Chinese, Pakistanis
individual	Victoria Burke, Dr. Jacobs
building	American Museum of Natural History

Which nouns are common? Which are proper?

       proper   common

6. Johann Gutenberg lived during the fifteenth century.

                 common   proper

7. This famous inventor was born in Germany.

   common   common   common

8. The man changed the production of books forever.

        proper   common   common

9. Before Gutenberg, pages were copied slowly by hand.

REMINDER

- A **concrete noun** names things that you can see, smell, taste, touch, or hear.
- An **abstract noun** names ideas, qualities, or feelings.
- A **common noun** names any person, place, thing, or idea.
- A **proper noun** names a particular person, place, thing, or idea.

Concrete Nouns	Abstract Nouns	Common Nouns	Proper Nouns
Aunt Sue	talent	teacher	Ms. Wright
town	bravery	month	March
beads	courage	museum	Hall of Fame

INDEPENDENT PRACTICE

A. Write each noun. Label it *concrete* or *abstract*.

1. The balloon rose with difficulty.   balloon — concrete, difficulty — abstract

2. Two pilots waved excitedly from the round platform.
pilots — concrete, platform — concrete

3. People were flying for the first time in history.
People — concrete, time — abstract, history — abstract

4. This amazing event occurred in Paris.   event — concrete, Paris — concrete

B. Write each noun. Label it *C* for common noun or *P* for proper noun.

5. Two brothers from France built the huge balloon.
brothers — C, France — P, balloon — C

6. Joseph Montgolfier and Jacques Montgolfier designed this craft.
Joseph Montgolfier — P, Jacques Montgolfier — P, craft — C

7. People from America to Asia entered the Age of Flight.
People — C, America — P, Asia — P, Age of Flight — P

Combining Sentences: Appositives

An **appositive** is a word or group of words that immediately follows a noun. Appositives identify the nouns they follow.

> Robin, **our class president,** planned the party.

Appositives can help you improve your writing. You can use an appositive to combine two choppy sentences into one sentence.

> Our summer party was a barbecue. It was great fun.

> Our summer party, **a barbecue,** was great fun.

Notice that an appositive is usually set off from the rest of the sentence by commas.

> Mr. McLean, Robin's father, furnished the chicken.
> The party had a theme, careers.

GUIDED PRACTICE

A. Use each noun and appositive in a sentence. Where would you place the commas? **Answers will vary; commas should set off each appositive.**

Example: Paulette — the fastest runner
Paulette, the fastest runner, lost the race.

1. My barber — a talkative person
2. Last Thursday — my birthday
3. Cal's terrier — Ruffles
4. The volleyball game — an exciting event

B. Combine each pair of sentences into a single sentence with an appositive. **Answers may vary.**

Example: Annie is my partner. She is building a new barn.
Annie, my partner, is building a new barn.

5. Mrs. Scott is Ken's mother. She is also my teacher.
6. My picture is in the local paper. The paper is the *Tribune*.
7. Harry is a disc jockey. Harry played my favorite record.
8. We're having tomato soup. It is my favorite.
5. Mrs. Scott, Ken's mother, is . . .
6. . . . the local paper, the *Tribune.*
7. Harry, a disc jockey, played . . .
8. . . . tomato soup, my favorite.

- An **appositive** is a word or group of words that immediately follows a noun and identifies or explains it.
- An appositive is usually set off from the rest of the sentence by commas.

Two Sentences: Dinosaurs were ancient land creatures. Dinosaurs are extinct.

appositive
One Sentence: Dinosaurs, **ancient land creatures,** are extinct.

INDEPENDENT PRACTICE

Combine each pair of sentences by making the underlined word or words an appositive. Use commas correctly.

Example: That creature is ninety feet long. It is a dinosaur.
That creature, a dinosaur, is ninety feet long.

1. Luis's sister is a scientist. She studies dinosaurs.
   Luis's sister, a scientist, studies dinosaurs.

2. Luis took Ali to his sister's office. Ali is his friend.
   Luis took Ali, his friend, to his sister's office.

3. Luis's sister was cleaning fossils. His sister is Rosa.
   Luis's sister, Rosa, was cleaning fossils.

4. She handled the fossils carefully. The fossils were bits of bone.
   She handled the fossils, bits of bone, carefully.

5. Rosa gave the boys a tour of the building. The building is a large museum.
   Rosa gave the boys a tour of the building, a large museum.

6. One exhibit was a dinosaur skeleton. It fascinated them.
   One exhibit, a dinosaur skeleton, fascinated them.

7. The skeleton was a brontosaur. It had a long neck and tail.
   The skeleton, a brontosaur, had a long neck and tail.

8. The skeleton Rosa works on is smaller. The skeleton is a triceratops.
   The skeleton Rosa works on, a triceratops, is smaller.

Often the verb in a sentence is made up of more than one word. A group of words that acts as a single verb is called a **verb phrase.** A verb phrase consists of one or more **helping verbs,** or **auxiliary verbs,** followed by a **main verb.** The main verb expresses the action or state of being.

Tiny water droplets **have been** <u>gathering</u>.

They **will** <u>form</u> a cloud.

Common Helping Verbs

be, am, is, are,	can, could
was, were, been	shall, should
has, have, had	will, would
does, do, did	might, may

Some verbs can be either main verbs or helping verbs.

HELPING

It **is** <u>snowing</u> outside.

I **have** <u>bought</u> new boots.

MAIN

The street <u>is</u> wet.

They <u>have</u> woolly linings.

Sometimes other words come between the parts of a verb phrase. What words interrupt the verb phrases below?

The sun **will** soon **have** <u>disappeared</u> behind the clouds.

Can you <u>see</u> any blue sky?

I **have** not <u>been</u> outside lately.

Don't <u>go</u> out in this weather.

Notice in the last two examples that the word *not* and its contraction, *n't,* are not part of the verb phrase.

GUIDED PRACTICE

Find the verb phrases in the sentences below. What are the main verbs? What are the helping verbs?

Example: Rain is not predicted for today.

main: *predicted* ***helping:*** *is*

1. I have checked the weather report.   have *checked*
2. Today should be clear and sunny.   should *be*
3. We can go to the park for our picnic.   can *go*
4. Large drops of rain have been falling for an hour.   have been *falling*
5. Don't you trust the weather report?   Do *trust*
6. The clouds and rain will not last long.   will *last*

- A **verb phrase** is a group of words that acts as a single verb.
- The **main verb** expresses the action or the state of being. The other verbs are **helping verbs** or **auxiliary verbs.**

auxiliary   main

The Empire State Building **has been struck** by lightning many times.

auxiliary   main

Did you ever **read** about that?

auxiliary main

Don't **borrow** my book about famous buildings.

INDEPENDENT PRACTICE

Write the verb phrase in each sentence.

Example: Scientists are collecting weather information.   **are collecting**

1. Meteorologists can often forecast weather correctly.   **can forecast**

2. However, the weather might change suddenly.   **might change**

3. We still do not completely understand it.   **do understand**

4. Meteorologists can't always predict the weather.   **can predict**

5. Their forecasts may sometimes be inaccurate.   **may be**

6. Forecasters can warn us about nearby storms, though.   **can warn**

7. Have you ever been caught in a sudden storm?   **Have been caught**

8. Storm clouds will usually appear very dark.   **will appear**

9. They can move quickly across the sky.   **can move**

10. You might have seen their unusual shapes.   **might have seen**

11. Do not go under a tree during a lightning storm.   **Do go**

12. You shouldn't stand in an open field, either.   **should stand**

13. Swimmers should immediately leave the water.   **should leave**

14. You would probably be safer in a car or building.   **would be**

15. People should listen to the weather report daily.   **should listen**

Be, have, and do are the most frequently used verbs in the English language. You have learned that you can use these verbs as main verbs or as helping verbs. There are no simple rules for forming the tenses of be, have, and do. You must memorize their forms.

Subject	be	have	do
Singular subjects:			
I	am, was	have, had	do, did
You	are, were	have, had	do, did
He, she, it (or singular noun)	is, was	has, had	does, did
Plural subjects:			
We	are, were	have, had	do, did
You	are, were	have, had	do, did
They (or plural noun)	are, were	have, had	do, did

GUIDED PRACTICE

Complete each sentence with the tense of the verb shown in parentheses.

Example: We _____ growing several kinds of beans.
(be − present)   *are*

1. We _____ green beans for dinner tonight.   (have − past)   **had**
2. They certainly _____ taste good.   (do − past)   **did**
3. I _____ picking fresh beans from the garden in our back yard.
   (be − present)   **am**
4. The green bean _____ a type of kidney bean.   (be − present)   **is**
5. Other varieties _____ lima beans, shell beans, and mung beans.
   (be − present)   **are**
6. We eat the seeds of most beans, but green beans also _____
   good-tasting pods.   (have − present)   **have**
7. Green beans _____ also called string beans.   (be − present)   **are**
8. At one time this popular vegetable actually _____ a string.
   (have − past)   **had**
9. The stringless bean _____ developed in the 1890's.   (be − past)   **was**
10. *Snap bean* _____ another name for a green bean.   (be − present)   **is**
11. A snap bean really _____ make a snapping sound.
    (do − present)   **does**

- Use the forms of *be, have,* and *do* as main verbs or as helping verbs. You must memorize their forms.

Subjects	Forms of *be*	Forms of *have*	Forms of *do*
I	am, was	have, had	do, did
he, she, it	is, was	has, had	does, did
singular nouns	is, was	has, had	does, did
we, you, they	are, were	have, had	do, did
plural nouns	are, were	have, had	do, did

INDEPENDENT PRACTICE

Write the correct form of the verb in parentheses to complete each sentence.

Example: Beth (has, have) a wonderful book of world records.   **has**

1. The largest lima bean (was, were) fourteen inches long.   was

2. Norma McCoy (is, are) the person who grew it.   is

3. How (did, do) she grow that lima bean?   did

4. I (am, is) not sure about that.   am

5. (Has, Have) you read about the largest carrot?   Have

6. Amazingly, it (have, had) a weight of eleven pounds.   had

7. I (does, do) not believe it!   do

8. The facts in this book (is, are) accurate.   are

9. (Is, Are) there record holders for the largest radish?   Are

10. Glen Tucker and Herbert Breslow (is, are) the record holders.   are

11. They (has, have) each grown a twenty-five-pound radish.   have

12. A man in Indiana (has, have) the record for squash.   has

13. Why (does, do) people grow these giant vegetables?   do

14. These people (has, have) probably grown them for contests.   have

Principal Parts

Every verb has four basic forms called **principal parts.** You use the principal parts to form all the tenses. Study the principal parts of the verbs in the chart below.

Principal Parts

Verb	Present participle	Past	Past participle
paint	(is) painting	painted	(has) painted
carry	(is) carrying	carried	(has) carried
love	(is) loving	loved	(has) loved
guess	(is) guessing	guessed	(has) guessed
enjoy	(is) enjoying	enjoyed	(has) enjoyed
plan	(is) planning	planned	(has) planned

GUIDED PRACTICE

What are the four principal parts of each of the following verbs?

1.	learn	(is) learning	learned	(has) learned
2.	cry	(is) crying	cried	(has) cried
3.	fuss	(is) fussing	fussed	(has) fussed
4.	hope	(is) hoping	hoped	(has) hoped
5.	knit	(is) knitting	knitted	(has) knitted

Forming the Perfect Tenses

You have already learned the three simple tenses — present, past, and future. There are also three **perfect tenses — present perfect, past perfect,** and **future perfect.** The three perfect tenses are made up of a form of the helping verb *have* and a past participle. The form of the helping verb shows the tense.

The Perfect Tenses

1. Use the **present perfect tense** to express an action that took place at an indefinite time in the past. The action may still be going on.

   Dr. Jiri **has conducted** the research.

2. Use the **past perfect tense** for an action in the past that was completed before another action took place.

   Dr. Jiri **had conducted** the research before the year ended.

3. Use the **future perfect tense** for an action that will be completed before another action in the future.

   Dr. Jiri **will have conducted** the research before the year ends.

What is the tense of the underlined verb in each of the following sentences?

1. Polio epidemics have become a thing of the past.   **present perfect**
2. Polio had threatened the lives of many people before a vaccine was discovered.   **past perfect**
3. A vaccine protects a person from a disease before the disease has started.   **present perfect**
4. Dr. Jonas Salk had already developed a successful vaccine when Dr. Albert Sabin produced an even more effective one.   **past perfect**

REMINDER

> • Every verb has four **principal parts.**
>
> | Verb | Present Participle | Past | Past Participle |
> |------|--------------------|------|-----------------|
> | try | (is) trying | tried | (has) tried |
> | plan | (is) planning | planned | (has) planned |
> | wipe | (is) wiping | wiped | (has) wiped |
>
> • The **perfect tenses** are made up of a form of *have* and the past participle.
>
> **Present Perfect Tense:** Doris **has studied** a chapter on vitamins. Her sisters **have studied** vitamins too.
> **Past Perfect Tense:** Doris **had** never **studied** this topic before.
> **Future Perfect Tense:** By 10:30 Doris **will have studied** hard.

INDEPENDENT PRACTICE

Write the tense of each underlined verb.

1. By next week our class will have learned about many different vitamins.   future perfect
2. Scientists have discovered vitamins only recently.   present perfect
3. I have started a report about James Lind.   present perfect
4. Lind had researched a disease.   past perfect
5. Over the centuries many sailors have suffered from this illness.   present perfect
6. Lind's studies had shown that lemon juice could prevent this disease.   past perfect
7. This illness has now become rare.   present perfect

Direct Objects

Every predicate contains a verb. Some predicates, however, need more than just a verb to complete the sentence.

> A dragonfly has.   *(Has what?)*

> A dragonfly has four fragile **wings.**

The additional words needed to complete the meaning of a sentence are called **complements.** Different verbs require different kinds of complements.

Some verbs require a **direct object** to receive the action. The direct object is always a noun or pronoun that answers the question *whom?* or *what?* after the verb.

> Beady eyes cover a dragonfly's **head.**   *(Cover what? head)*

> Dragonflies do not harm **people.**   *(Harm whom? people)*

A sentence may contain a compound direct object.

> Dragonflies eat **mosquitoes** and other **insects.**

Indirect Objects

The direct object receives the action, and the **indirect object** tells who or what was affected by the action.

>   **indirect**   **direct**
> I showed *Vince* the **fireflies.**

>   **indirect**   **direct**
> The fireflies gave *us* a good **show.**

Only sentences with direct objects can have indirect objects. To determine whether a sentence has an indirect object, first find the direct object. The indirect object always comes before the direct object.

Indirect objects answer the questions *to or for whom?* and *to or for what?* Nouns or pronouns with *to* and *for* can replace indirect objects. If a word follows *to* or *for,* however, it is not an indirect object.

> I showed the fireflies *to Vince.*

> The fireflies gave a show *for us.*

Like direct objects, indirect objects can be compound.

>   **indirect indirect**   **direct**
> The fireflies gave *Vince* and *me* a good **show.**

Find each object in the sentences below. Is the object direct or indirect?

                    I.O.   D.O.

1.   Ms. Jackson taught my science class interesting facts about insects.

         I.O.   D.O.

2.   I asked her some questions about spiders.

          I.O.   I.O. D.O.

3.   She lent Mark and me a book of photographs of spider webs.

                          I.O.   D.O.   D.O.

4.   Each type of spider gives its web a different shape and design.

REMINDER

> • A **direct object** tells *who* or *what* receives the action of a transitive verb.
>
> I saw **Jennifer** and **Tracy** in the library.   *(saw whom?)*
>
> They were reading a **book** about insects.   *(were reading what?)*
>
> • An **indirect object** tells *who* or *what* was affected by the action.
>
> My parents bought my **brother** and **me** an ant farm.   *(bought for whom?)*
>
> We gave the **ants** some sugar.   *(gave to what?)*

INDEPENDENT PRACTICE

Write each underlined object. Then label it *direct* or *indirect*.

1.   Rona showed <u>Hans</u> and <u>me</u> her science <u>project</u> on crickets.
   Hans — indirect, me — indirect, project — direct

2.   She had given <u>it</u> an interesting <u>title</u>. **it — indirect, title — direct**

3.   She thanked <u>us</u> for our interest in it. **us — direct**

4.   Later, Rona showed the <u>class</u> a cricket <u>cage</u>.
   class — indirect, cage — direct

Although action verbs can have objects, linking verbs cannot. A linking verb connects the subject with a word that identifies or describes it. A noun that renames the subject is called a **predicate noun** or **predicate nominative.**

DIRECT OBJECT: This book describes funny **creatures.**

PREDICATE NOUN: *The Hobbit* is its **title.**

An adjective that follows a linking verb and describes, or modifies, the subject is called a **predicate adjective.**

PREDICATE ADJECTIVE: The story sounds **wonderful.**

Predicate nouns and predicate adjectives may be compound.

Hobbits resemble English **countrymen** and **rabbits.**

They look **short, stout,** and **hairy.**

GUIDED PRACTICE

What are the predicate nouns and predicate adjectives in the sentences below?

Example: J. R. R. Tolkien was an English scholar and writer.
scholar, writer; p.n.

1. He became famous for *The Hobbit.*   **famous, p.a.**
2. *The Hobbit* was originally a story for Tolkien's children.   **story, p.n.**
3. It is an introduction to *The Lord of the Rings*, a series of books about hobbits.   **introduction, p.n.**
4. It grew popular with children and adults everywhere.   **popular, p.a.**
5. Hobbits are industrious and good-natured.   **industrious, good-natured; p.a.**
6. Their homes are comfortable holes in the ground.   **holes, p.n.**
7. The main hobbit's name is Bilbo Baggins.   **Bilbo Baggins, p.n.**
8. He is odd but charming.   **odd, charming; p.a.**
9. Throughout the books, the hobbits' world becomes very detailed.   **detailed, p.a.**
10. There are maps, illustrations, and even a made-up language of the elves.   **maps, illustrations, language; p.n.**

REMINDER

- A **predicate noun** follows a linking verb. It identifies or renames the subject.

   The Call of the Wild is an exciting **novel**.

- A **predicate adjective** follows a linking verb. It describes the subject.

   The story was **realistic** and **suspenseful**.

INDEPENDENT PRACTICE

Write the underlined words. Label them *predicate noun* or *predicate adjective*.

Example: The author is <u>Jack London</u>.   **Jack London — predicate noun**

1. *The Call of the Wild* is a great <u>book</u>.   book — predicate noun

2. The setting is <u>Alaska</u> and <u>Canada</u> during the Klondike gold rush.
   Alaska — predicate noun, Canada — predicate noun

3. Buck, a dog, is the main <u>character</u>.   character — predicate noun

4. One of Buck's owners is <u>unkind</u>.   unkind — predicate adjective

5. Buck becomes <u>thin</u> and <u>weak</u> during his stay with this owner.
   thin — predicate adjective, weak — predicate adjective

6. A man named John Thornton feels <u>sorry</u> for Buck.
   sorry — predicate adjective

7. He becomes the dog's new <u>master</u>.   master — predicate noun

8. After Thornton dies, Buck becomes <u>free</u>.   free — predicate adjective

9. Jack London was a good <u>writer</u>.   writer — predicate noun

10. Like some of his heroes, he was once an <u>adventurer</u> in the
    Klondike.   adventurer — predicate noun

11. As a writer, he became <u>famous</u> and <u>well-to-do</u>.
    famous — predicate adjective, well-to-do — predicate adjective

12. Other novels of his are *White Fang* and *The Sea Wolf*.
    White Fang — predicate noun, *The Sea Wolf* — predicate noun

opyright © Houghton Mifflin Company. All rights reserved.

LANGUAGE AND USAGE   172

In sentences with transitive verbs, the subject performs the action, and the object receives the action.

When the subject is the doer of the action, the verb is in the **active voice.** An active verb sends its action forward to the object.

ACTIVE VOICE: Zebras **surrounded** the bus.

Sometimes the action of a sentence goes the other way. Then the subject becomes the receiver of the action rather than the doer.

When the subject receives the action, the verb is in the **passive voice.** A passive verb sends its action back to the subject.

PASSIVE VOICE: The bus **was surrounded** by zebras.

When you switch a verb from the active voice to the passive voice, the sentence changes in several ways.

1. The verb changes from the past to the past participle form, and a form of *be* comes before it.

    ACTIVE: Mrs. Juru **led** the safari.

    PASSIVE: The safari **was led** by Mrs. Juru.

2. The object of the active verb becomes the subject in the sentence with the passive verb.

    ACTIVE: Her son **drove** the bus.

    PASSIVE: The bus **was driven** by her son.

3. The subject of the sentence with the active verb follows the word *by* in the sentence with the passive verb.

    ACTIVE: Mr. Watts **spotted** a giraffe.

    PASSIVE: A giraffe **was spotted** by Mr. Watts.

A sentence with a verb in the passive voice does not always show the doer of the action.

Many wild animals **were photographed** by our group.
Many wild animals **were photographed.**

Remember that intransitive verbs and linking verbs do not have objects. Therefore, these verbs are never in the passive voice.

GUIDED PRACTICE

Is each verb in the active voice or the passive voice?

1. Very few wild animals bother the giraffe. active
2. A giraffe is protected by the color pattern of its coat. passive
3. White lines separate the yellowish-brown coat into spots. active
4. Against leafy trees the giraffe is hidden by this pattern. passive

REMINDER

- When the subject does the action, the verb is in the **active voice.**
- When the subject receives the action, the verb is in the **passive voice.**

Active Voice	**Passive Voice**
Many tourists **visit** East Africa.	East Africa **is visited** by many tourists.
They **may see** cheetahs there.	Cheetahs **may be seen** there.

INDEPENDENT PRACTICE

Underline the verb in each sentence. Then label the verb *active* or *passive.*

Example: Antelope are hunted by cheetahs.   **passive**

1. Cheetahs hunt antelope.   active
2. Cheetahs run faster than any other animal.   active
3. Many cheetahs were captured in the past.   passive
4. Some of the cheetahs were trained.   passive
5. People tamed these animals.   active
6. Today cheetahs and other wild cats are protected.   passive
7. Female cheetahs protect their cubs from lions.   active
8. These animals are watched closely by some photographers.   passive
9. Many wonderful pictures have been taken of cheetahs.   passive
10. The animals are watched by tourists too.   passive

Subject-Verb Agreement

Subjects and verbs must always agree in number. Use a singular verb with a singular subject and a plural verb with a plural subject. Note that the subject of a sentence can be a noun or a pronoun. Singular subject pronouns are *I, you, he, she,* and *it.* Plural subject pronouns are *we, you,* and *they.*

SINGULAR

The **piano is** out of tune.
He plays the drums.

PLURAL

The **pianos are** out of tune.
They play the drums.

Making verbs agree with compound subjects can be tricky.

1. Use a plural verb with subjects joined by *and.*

    My school's **orchestra** and **band have** different instruments.

2. Use a singular verb with singular subjects joined by *or* or *nor.*

    The **piano** or **harp is** the prettiest instrument.

    Neither **she** nor **he plays** in the orchestra.

3. Use a plural verb with plural subjects joined by *or* or *nor.*

    Saxophones or **clarinets are** common in a band.

4. If a compound subject has *both* singular and plural nouns joined by *or* or *nor,* use a verb that agrees with the noun closer to it.

    Neither **kettledrums** nor the **xylophone is** in the band.
    The **bass drum, snare drum,** or **cymbals keep** the rhythm.

GUIDED PRACTICE

Choose the correct form of the verb to complete each sentence.

Example: The earliest horns (was, were) long, straight tubes.   *were*

1. Today, instrument makers (coils, coil) the tubes of metal.
2. They (handles, handle) these instruments more easily than the earlier horns.
3. At first, neither trumpets nor other horns (was, were) played with valves.
4. Nowadays the trumpet, the trombone, and the tuba (has, have) three valves.
5. French horns (has, have) three or more valves.

- Subjects and verbs must **agree** in number.
- Use a plural verb with compound subjects joined by *and.*
- With compound subjects joined by *or* or *nor*, use a verb that agrees with the closer subject.

Singular Subjects: Ken likes the guitar. He plays the banjo.

Plural Subjects: Those boys like the guitar. They play the banjo.

Compound Subjects: Melinda and Julie play the harp.
    Neither Jenny nor her parents play the guitar.
    Either the guitars or the banjo is out of tune.

INDEPENDENT PRACTICE

Write the verb in parentheses that agrees with the underlined subject.

Example: Most guitars (has, have) six strings.   **have**

1. Several stringed instruments (is, are) played by plucking.   are

2. A pick or the fingers (pluck, plucks) the strings.   pluck

3. The mandolin and the lute (has, have) pear-shaped bodies.   have

4. Between four and nine strings (stretch, stretches) the length of the banjo.   stretch

5. The mandolin (has, have) four pairs of strings.   has

6. Neither banjos nor mandolins usually (belong, belongs) in orchestras.   belong

7. The birthplace of guitars (is, are) probably Spain.   is

8. The guitar usually (has, have) six strings.   has

9. Its sides (curve, curves) inward to form a waist.   curve

10. Lutes (was, were) popular in the sixteenth and seventeenth centuries in Europe.   were

11. Neither the modern lute's strings nor its neck (is, are) the same as the early lute's.   is

12. Stringed instruments (seem, seems) almost as old as music itself.   seem

Some verbs do not show action. They show what the subject is or is like. Verbs called **being verbs** show a state of being.

Mr. Wong **is** the principal.   He **seems** kind.   He **is** here.

A being verb is often a **linking verb.** It links the subject of the sentence with a word in the predicate that tells more about it.

This newspaper *feels* damp.   It *became* wet in the rain.

Common Being and Linking Verbs				
am	was	be	become	feel
is	were	being	look	taste
are	seem	been	appear	smell

Linking verbs link the subject with a word in the predicate. The word can be a **predicate noun** or a **predicate adjective.** A predicate noun renames the subject. A predicate adjective describes the subject. Linking verbs never have direct objects.

PREDICATE NOUNS: Don **is** our **leader.** (Don = leader)

He **has become** my **friend.** (He = friend)

PREDICATE ADJECTIVES: Ms. Hill **was friendly.**

She **appeared shy** to strangers.

GUIDED PRACTICE

What is the linking verb in each sentence? What is the predicate noun or predicate adjective?

Example: The Black Hills are really mountains.   *are   mountains*

1. Thunderhead Mountain is <u>part</u> of the Black Hills.
2. Someday the mountain top <u>will become</u> a huge <u>statue</u>.
3. The statue <u>will be</u> a <u>profile</u> of Chief Crazy Horse.
4. Chief Crazy Horse <u>was</u> a Sioux Indian <u>chief</u>.
5. The statue <u>is</u> <u>rough</u> now.

- A **being verb** shows a state of being.
- A being verb is called a **linking verb** when it links the subject with a word in the predicate.
- A **predicate noun** renames or identifies the subject.
- A **predicate adjective** describes the subject.

Linking Verbs: A popular newspaper section **is** the comics .

predicate noun

Comic strips **have become** popular .

predicate adjective

INDEPENDENT PRACTICE

Write the linking verb in each sentence.

Example: Comic strips are a big part of many newspapers. — **are**

1. My aunt is the author of a comic strip. — **is**
2. Her office is a busy and colorful place. — **is**
3. Her special ink smells funny. — **smells**
4. The characters in her strip are little animals. — **are**
5. Some of them look humorous. — **look**
6. My aunt's comic strip has been very successful. — **has been**
7. Comic strips can be serious too. — **can be**
8. I am fond of both kinds of comics. — **am**
9. The history of comics seems exciting. — **seems**
10. Comics once became weapons in a newspaper battle. — **became**
11. Joseph Pulitzer was the first to publish color funnies. — **was**
12. The sales of his newspaper were high. — **were**
13. W. R. Hearst felt jealous of Pulitzer's success. — **felt**
14. Sunday funnies soon became part of his papers too. — **became**
15. Now comics have become serious business for publishers. — **have become**

Pronouns and Antecedents

Pronouns, such as *I, her,* or *they,* take the place of nouns and help make sentences smoother and more direct.

> Ned found **his** tools and put **them** in **his** toolbox.

Pronouns get most of their meaning from the nouns they replace. The noun that a pronoun replaces is its **antecedent.** An antecedent usually appears in a sentence before a pronoun and names the person, place, thing, or idea to which the pronoun refers.

> **Ned** put the finishing touches on the table **he** was making.

> Ned rubbed the **wood** with oil until **it** gleamed.

A pronoun and its antecedent may appear in separate sentences.

> **Ned** had carefully inspected the wood for this table.
> **He** had selected the finest oak.

A pronoun can have more than one noun as an antecedent.

> **Ned** and his **brother** work together; **they** make furniture.

A noun can also serve as the antecedent for more than one pronoun.

> **Ned** was fifteen years old when **he** sold **his** first piece.

Sometimes an antecedent follows the pronoun rather than comes before it.

> When **it** is finished, this **table** will bring a good price.

GUIDED PRACTICE

Find the antecedent of each underlined pronoun. The antecedent may be in a different sentence.

Example: Melissa found an old diary in <u>her</u> home. *Melissa*

1. <u>It</u> dated back to the nineteenth century. diary

2. A young boy had written the journal about <u>his</u> family. boy

3. <u>His</u> father was a hard-working logger at a lumber mill. boy

4. The loggers worked carefully, and <u>they</u> cut only older trees. loggers

5. <u>They</u> would then replace the newly cut trees with saplings. loggers

LANGUAGE AND USAGE   179

- A **pronoun** is a word that takes the place of one or more nouns.
- The noun that a pronoun replaces is called its **antecedent.**

For **Mia** to win a set of tennis, **she** had to win six games.

Both Mia and Don wanted to win the match. **They** had trained very hard.

INDEPENDENT PRACTICE

Write the antecedent or antecedents for each underlined pronoun.

Example: Mia played a match against <u>her</u> friend Don.   **Mia**

1. Mia and Don were friends, and <u>they</u> loved tennis.   Mia, Don

2. Don's parents watched <u>their</u> son enter the stadium.   parents

3. The officials took <u>their</u> places.   officials

4. The usher told Don's parents, "<u>You</u> should find <u>your</u> seats."   parents

5. "<u>I</u> hope that Don isn't too nervous," said Don's mother.   mother

6. The first game began, and Mia won <u>it</u> easily.   game

7. In fact, Mia was surprised that <u>she</u> won the first set.   Mia

8. Don lost because <u>he</u> played such a careless game.   Don

9. Don hit one ball wildly, and <u>it</u> landed in the stands.   ball

10. Don tossed the racket and damaged <u>its</u> head.   racket

11. Don's father calmed <u>his</u> son.   father

12. Eight more games followed, and Don won six of <u>them</u>.   games

13. Now that <u>they</u> were tied, the opponents played harder.   opponents

14. Soon Mia had a one-game edge, and <u>she</u> was serving.   Mia

15. Mia's mother leaped to <u>her</u> feet when Mia won the match.   mother

Pronouns in Compound Subjects and Objects

You must be careful about which form of a pronoun you use in a compound subject or a compound object. The choice may be clearer if you separate the parts of the compound.

> Nelly went to rehearsal. I went to rehearsal. (not *me went*)
> Nelly and **I** went to rehearsal.

> Li taught Jim a step. Li taught her a step. (not *taught she*)
> Li taught Jim and **her** a step.

GUIDED PRACTICE

A. Choose the correct pronoun.

Example: Some friends and (I, me) went to a performance by the Alvin Ailey American Dance Theater. *I*

1. The company thrilled the rest of the audience and (we, us).
2. Carlos and (I, me) especially enjoyed Donna Woods in "Cry."
3. Carlos had seen (she, her) and Judith Jamison in that dance.
4. (He, Him) and Victoria also saw Judith Jamison on Broadway.
5. (They, Them) and (I, me) consider her a great dancer.

GUIDED PRACTICE

B. Write the sentences, using correct pronouns.

6. The other dancers and (I, me) got ready for the show.

   _____

7. The director gave the stage crew and (we, us) instructions.

   _____

8. A dresser helped Nelly and (I, me) with our costumes.

   _____

9. (She, Her) and (I, me) took our places in the wings.

   _____

10. The audience loved the other dancers and (we, us).

    _____

11. The dancers thanked (they, them) and the director with bows.

    _____

REMINDER

- To choose the correct pronoun in a compound subject or compound object, separate the parts of the compound.

  My sister loves camping. **I** love camping.

  My sister and **I** love camping.

  My parents took **her** camping. My parents took **me** camping.

  My parents took **her** and **me** camping.

INDEPENDENT PRACTICE

Write the correct pronoun in parentheses to complete each sentence.

Example: My parents took my friend and (we, us) camping.   **us**

1. My family and (I, me) all had jobs on the camping trip.   I

2. (They, Them) and (I, me) shared the work fairly.   They, I

3. Greg helped Elsa and (I, me) gather firewood.   me

4. (He, Him) and Elsa gathered kindling while I split logs.   He

5. Then (we, us) and my parents set up the tents.   we

6. (They, Them) and Greg slept in the bigger one.   They

7. Elsa and (I, me) assembled our tent.   I

8. My parents helped (she, her) and (I, me).   her, me

9. Greg just watched (they, them) and (we, us).   them, us

10. Later my mother took (he, him) and Elsa to the lake.   him

11. My mother and (they, them) wanted to swim.   they

12. She asked my father and (I, me) to start the campfire.   me

13. (He, Him) and (I, me) stacked the wood carefully.   He, I

14. My mother complimented (we, us) on our great fire.   us

15. (She, Her) and my father made the stew.   She

16. Greg and I didn't cook, but (we, us) washed the dishes.   we

17. My parents and (we, us) rested by the fire.   we

18. Later (they, them) and (we, us) put out the fire.   they, we

When you ask a question, you often begin it with a type of pronoun called an **interrogative pronoun.**

> **What** is the name of the newspaper?
> **Who** is the newspaper editor?
> **Which** of the reporters is assigned to this story?
> **Whom** did Connie interview?
> **Whose** is this copy?

If you have trouble deciding whether to use *who* or *whom* in a question, try turning the question into a statement. If the pronoun is a predicate pronoun, use *who*. If it is an object, use *whom*.

> **Who** is the newspaper editor?
> The newspaper editor is **who**?   *(predicate pronoun)*
> **Whom** did Connie interview?
> Connie interviewed **whom**?   *(direct object)*

Be careful not to confuse the interrogative pronoun *whose* with the contraction *who's*.

> INTERROGATIVE PRONOUN: Whose is this copy?
> CONTRACTION: Who's reading that copy?   *(Who is)*

GUIDED PRACTICE

A. What is the interrogative pronoun in each sentence?

Example: Who advises the school newspaper staff?   *Who*

1. Who are the reporters?   Who
2. Russ, what are you writing for the newspaper?   what
3. Whom did you ask for information?   Whom
4. Whose are these notes?   Whose
5. Rona, which is your notebook?   which

B. Choose the correct word to complete each sentence.

Example: (Who, Whom) takes pictures for the newspaper?
    Who

6. (Whose, Who's) is that camera?
7. (Who, Whom) did Jamie photograph for this month's issue?
8. (Who, Whom) develops the film?
9. (Whose, Who's) in the photograph on page eight?

- Use the **interrogative pronoun**s *what, which, who, whom,* and *whose* in questions.
- Use *who* as a subject. Use *whom* as an object.
- Do not confuse *whose* with the contraction *who's.*

> **What** must be done for this party?
> **Which** of us will send the invitations?
> **Who** can bring napkins and paper plates?
> **Whom** have you asked for help?
> **Whose** are these decorations?

INDEPENDENT PRACTICE

Write the correct word in parentheses to complete each sentence.

Example: (Who, Whom) wants to have a party?   **Who**

1. (Whose, Who's) is the best house for the party?   Whose
2. (Whose, Who's) is the largest living room?   Whose
3. (Who, Whom) should we invite?   Whom
4. (Whose, Who's) the funniest person in our class?   Who's
5. (Who, Whom) can bring a camera?   Who
6. (Whose, Who's) is the best cassette tape collection?   Whose
7. (Who, Whom) can we ask for food?   Whom
8. (Who, Whom) will pay for it?   Who
9. (Whose, Who's) are the best recipes?   Whose
10. (Who, Whom) shall we ask for decorating ideas?   Whom
11. (Whose, Who's) in charge of the telephone calls?   Who's
12. (Who, Whom) needs a list of names and phone numbers?   Who
13. (Who, Whom) should we call first?   Whom
14. (Who, Whom) has the most time today?   Who
15. (Whose, Who's) a good organizer?   Who's
16. (Whose, Who's) in charge of cleanup?   Who's

Some pronouns are used to point out particular persons and things. These are called **demonstrative pronouns.**

> **This** is a map of New York City.
> Is **that** Central Park?

There are four demonstrative pronouns: *this, that, these,* and *those. This* and *these* point out persons and things that are nearby. *That* and *those* point out persons or things that are farther away. Demonstrative pronouns agree in number with the nouns to which they refer.

> SINGULAR: this (near)   that (far)
> PLURAL: these (near)   those (far)

> **This** is **Times Square.**
> **These** are the famous neon **lights** of Broadway.
> Is **that** the **Brooklyn Bridge** over there?
> **Those** are the twin **towers** of the World Trade Center.

The words *this, that, these,* and *those* can also be used before nouns. When they are used with nouns, these words function as adjectives rather than as pronouns.

> DEMONSTRATIVE PRONOUN: These are busy streets.
> DEMONSTRATIVE ADJECTIVE: These streets are busy.

GUIDED PRACTICE

Choose the demonstrative pronoun that correctly completes each sentence. Which noun in the sentence is pointed out by the demonstrative pronoun?

Example: (This, These) is Peachtree Street, the major street in downtown Atlanta.   *This   Peachtree Street*

1.   Is (that, those) the site of the annual Peachtree Road Race?

2.   (This, These) was the birthplace of Martin Luther King, Jr.

3.   (These, Those) are the buildings of the Atlanta University Center on this street.

4.   (This, That) is the stadium of the Atlanta Braves on the other side of the highway.

5.   (That, Those) are cheers from enthusiastic baseball fans in the stands.

> - **Demonstrative pronouns** point out particular persons and things.
> - Use *this* and *these* for things that are close by.
> - Use *that* and *those* for things that are farther away.
> - Demonstrative pronouns must agree in number with the nouns to which they refer.
>
> **This** is the Mississippi River.   **That** is New Orleans in the distance.
> **These** are the famous riverbanks.   **Those** are historic houses on the shore.

INDEPENDENT PRACTICE

Write the correct demonstrative pronoun in parentheses to complete each sentence.

Example: (This, These) is Jackson Square.   **This**

1. (This, These) is the well-known French Quarter.   This
2. (This, These) is the oldest section in New Orleans.   This
3. (This, That) is an information center over there.   That
4. (This, These) are the famous balconies.   These
5. (This, These) are a trademark of New Orleans.   These
6. (This, That) is Canal Street that we are crossing.   This
7. (This, These) certainly is a wide roadway.   This
8. Are (these, those) the Pontalba Buildings across the way?   those
9. (That, Those) are the nation's oldest apartments.   Those
10. (These, Those) are new shops on the other side of the street.   Those
11. Is (this, that) the Garden District across the river?   that
12. (This, These) are some of the city's finest homes.   These
13. Are (these, those) magnolia trees behind the wall?   those
14. (This, These) are magnificent gardens!   These
15. (This, That) is Audubon Park in the distance.   That
16. Is (that, those) the largest park in the city?   that
17. Is (this, that) a good restaurant over there?   that
18. (This, These) is the best French restaurant in the city.   This

To whom do the subjects of these sentences refer?

Someone has started the fireworks.   **Everyone** watches the sky.

These pronouns do not refer to definite persons or things. They do not have clear antecedents because the persons or things they refer to are unknown. Pronouns such as these are called **indefinite pronouns.**

Indefinite Pronouns

Singular			Plural	Singular or plural
anybody	everyone	nothing	both	all
anyone	everything	one	few	any
anything	neither	somebody	many	most
each	nobody	someone	several	none
either	no one	something		some
everybody				

Notice that *all, any, most, none,* and *some* can be singular or plural, depending upon how they are used. These pronouns are plural when they refer to things that can be counted. They are singular when they refer to things that cannot be counted.

SINGULAR: **Most** of the **town** closes on the Fourth of July.
PLURAL: **Most** of the **stores** close on the Fourth of July.

When words like *all, most,* or *each* are used before nouns, they function as adjectives, not as indefinite pronouns.

INDEFINITE PRONOUN: **Some** carried flags in the parade.
ADJECTIVE: **Some** children carried flags in the parade.

When an indefinite pronoun is the subject of a sentence, the verb must agree with it.

SINGULAR: **Everyone enjoys** the Fourth of July celebration.
PLURAL: **Many** of the people **cheer** at the last burst of fireworks.

Indefinite pronouns can be antecedents for personal pronouns.

SINGULAR: **Each** of the countries in the world has **its** own holidays.
PLURAL: **Some** have holidays in honor of **their** independence.

Use the chart of indefinite pronouns to remind yourself which ones are singular, plural, or both.

GUIDED PRACTICE

Find the indefinite pronoun and choose the verb or the pronoun that agrees with it.

1. In China, <u>all</u> of the people (celebrates, <u>celebrate</u>) (its, <u>their</u>) birthdays at New Year's.
2. <u>Everyone</u> (<u>exchanges</u>, exchange) gifts, such as flowers, food, or silks.
3. <u>Many</u> (gives, <u>give</u>) shoes, symbols of a prosperous year, to (its, <u>their</u>) relatives.
4. In the United States, <u>one</u> usually (<u>spends</u>, spend) New Year's Eve with friends.
5. On New Year's Day, <u>no one</u> (<u>works</u>, work) or (<u>goes</u>, go) to school.

REMINDER

- **Indefinite pronouns** do not refer to definite persons or things.
- When indefinite pronouns act as subjects, the verbs must agree with them.
- When they act as antecedents, pronouns must agree with them.

Singular:	**Everybody** <u>has</u> some kind of hobby.
	All of this area <u>is</u> filled with birds.
Plural:	**Many** of my friends <u>enjoy</u> <u>their</u> clubs.
	All of the bird-watching clubs <u>sponsor</u> outings.

INDEPENDENT PRACTICE

Label each underlined indefinite pronoun *singular* or *plural*.

1. <u>Few</u> of us are knowledgeable about birds. _____plural_____
2. <u>Most</u> of the members have difficulty identifying sparrows. _____plural_____
3. Certainly <u>no one</u> recognizes these warblers. _____singular_____
4. Does <u>anyone</u> know the name of this sea bird? _____singular_____

Write the verb or pronoun in parentheses that agrees with each underlined indefinite pronoun.

5. <u>Few</u> of the bird watchers (imitates, imitate) birdcalls. _____imitate_____
6. (Has, Have) <u>anybody</u> made a recording of a birdcall? _____Has_____
7. (Does, Do) <u>any</u> of the professional organizations give recordings to (its, their) members? _____Do, their_____

You have learned that prepositional phrases are used as single words. A prepositional phrase that functions as an adjective is called an **adjective phrase.**

ADJECTIVE: The first wallpaper was **Chinese.**
ADJECTIVE PHRASE: The first wallpaper was **from China.**

An adjective phrase, like an adjective, modifies a noun or a pronoun. It tells *which one* or *what kind.*

Woven fabrics were some **of the first wall coverings** .

Wallpaper was a cheap substitute **for woven wall hangings** .

You already know that one prepositional phrase can follow another. When that happens, the second adjective phrase often modifies the object of the first adjective phrase.

Birds or flowers decorated much **of the paper** **from China** .

Sometimes two adjective phrases follow each other and modify the same word.

Soon wallpaper **from France** **with black designs** appeared.

GUIDED PRACTICE

Which noun or pronoun is modified by each underlined adjective phrase?

Example: In 1867, C. Latham Sholes read a magazine article about a machine for printing letters.
article   machine

1. Many attempts at this type of invention had already failed. **attempts, type**
2. A typing machine with accuracy and speed had not yet been developed. **machine**
3. In 1868, Sholes and two other men patented a machine with eleven keys. **machine**
4. All of the letters on this typewriter were capitals. **All, letters**
5. Sholes built dozens of typewriters, and each time he made improvements on the machine. **dozens, improvements**

- A prepositional phrase that modifies a noun or a pronoun is an **adjective phrase.**

Adjective Phrases: The title **of the movie** was *City Lights.*

The audience **in the theater on Kings Highway** loved it.

INDEPENDENT PRACTICE

Write each underlined adjective phrase and the noun or the pronoun that it modifies.

Example: I enjoy films <u>with many funny scenes</u>.
with many funny scenes — films

1. Ms. Keller's class watched films <u>of the early 1900's</u>.
   of the early 1900's — films

2. The class saw movies <u>by Chaplin, Keaton, and others</u>.
   by Chaplin, Keaton, and others — movies

3. Many <u>of the early films</u> <u>without sound</u> are masterpieces.
   of the early films — Many; without sound — films

4. Charlie Chaplin made brilliant movies <u>about a lovable tramp</u>.
   about a lovable tramp — movies

5. Pianists <u>in theaters</u> provided much <u>of the music</u>.
   in theaters — Pianists; of the music — much

6. Lon Chaney was a silent actor <u>with great talent</u>.
   with great talent — actor

7. The introduction <u>of movies</u> <u>with sound</u> ended some careers.
   of movies — introduction; with sound — movies

8. Many actors <u>of the silent movie age</u> retired early.
   of the silent movie age — actors

A prepositional phrase that functions as an adverb is called an **adverb phrase.**

ADVERB: Let's meet **outside.**
ADVERB PHRASE: Let's meet **outside the terminal.**

Like adverbs, adverb phrases modify verbs, adjectives, or other adverbs.

VERB: We will travel **with a tour.**

ADJECTIVE: This tour is famous **for its careful planning.**

ADVERB: Have you ever traveled far **from home**?

Also like adverbs, adverb phrases tell *how, when, where,* or *to what extent.*

The tour will travel **by plane.** *(how)*
The plane will leave **in the morning.** *(when)*
Our tour will stop **in many cities.** *(where)*
We will be traveling **for a long time.** *(to what extent)*

Adverb phrases can occur anywhere in a sentence.

The plane was waiting **on the runway.**
At the gate stood many people.
I checked my luggage **at the counter** and boarded the plane.

More than one adverb phrase can modify the same word.

After a few minutes, we stepped **onto the plane.**

GUIDED PRACTICE

Which verb, adjective, or adverb is modified by each underlined adverb phrase?

Example: We arrived <u>in Paris</u> early <u>in April</u>. *arrived early*

1. We strolled <u>by the river</u> and spent days <u>in the museums</u>. **strolled, spent**
2. Paris is beautiful <u>in the spring</u>. **beautiful**
3. <u>After a few days</u>, we drove <u>through the Pyrenees mountains to Spain</u>. **drove**
4. The villages looked tiny <u>from high</u> <u>in the mountains</u>. **tiny, high**
5. We drove <u>to the shore</u> and ate seafood <u>at a seaside cafe</u>. **drove, ate**

- A prepositional phrase that modifies a verb, an adjective, or another adverb is an **adverb phrase.**

The Blackstones traveled **by train.** (modifies verb *traveled*)

The train was full **of tourists.** (modifies adjective *full*)

They arrived early **in the morning.** (modifies adverb *early*)

INDEPENDENT PRACTICE

Write each underlined adverb phrase and the word or words that it modifies.

Example: The Blackstones traveled to California by car.

to California, by car — traveled

1. On June 6, 1987, they traveled across the Golden Gate Bridge.
On June 6, 1987, across the Golden Gate Bridge — traveled

2. The Blackstones traveled from San Francisco to Los Angeles.
from San Francisco, to Los Angeles — traveled

3. On the way, they drove through the San Joaquin Valley.
On the way, through the San Joaquin Valley — drove

4. The Blackstones stayed in the area for many days.
in the area, for many days — stayed

5. The San Joaquin Valley is famous for its lovely produce.
for its lovely produce — famous

6. Large truck farms thrive not far from the coast.
from the coast — far

7. They have been producing vegetables and cotton for many years.
for many years — have been producing

8. During most seasons the crops grow well in this central valley.
During most seasons, in this central valley — grow

An **infinitive** is made up of the word *to* and the base form of the verb.

> Paul wants **to leave.**   It is necessary **to go.**

You can use infinitives as nouns, adjectives, or adverbs.

Uses for an Infinitive	
As a noun:	
subject	**To leave** would be rude.
direct object	I want **to leave.**
predicate noun	His decision is **to leave.**
object of a preposition	I want nothing except **to leave.**
As an adjective:	
modifies a noun	Now is the time **to leave.**
modifies a pronoun	She is someone **to follow.**
As an adverb:	
modifies a verb	**To leave,** use the back door.
modifies an adjective	We are ready **to leave.**
modifies an adverb	He is well enough **to travel.**

Be careful not to confuse infinitives with prepositional phrases that begin with *to.*

> INFINITIVE: Is this the road **to take**?
> PREPOSITIONAL PHRASE: Is this the road **to the store**?

GUIDED PRACTICE

Find each infinitive. Is it used as a noun, an adjective, or an adverb?

Example: To study, you may go to a quiet library.
> *To study — **adverb***

1. Do you want <u>to study</u>?   noun
2. When you need <u>to concentrate</u>, look for peace and quiet.   noun
3. Many people go to some quiet corner of their home.   none
4. Soft music may make it easier <u>to concentrate</u>.   adverb
5. The best time <u>to study</u> is before you become tired.   adjective
6. <u>To learn</u>, you should organize the information.   adverb
7. <u>To summarize</u> is helpful to most people.   noun

- An **infinitive** is formed with the word *to* and the base form of the verb.
- An infinitive can be used as a noun, an adjective, or an adverb.

Noun:	Dana likes **to read**.
Adjective:	Novels are good books **to read**.
Adverb:	Most newspapers are easy **to read**.

INDEPENDENT PRACTICE

Write the infinitives in these sentences. Write *none* if the sentence does not have an infinitive.

Example: A good book can be a way to explore.　　　<u>**to explore**</u>

1. To communicate is the aim of most authors.　　<u>**To communicate**</u>

2. To read is a way to grow.　　<u>**To read, to grow**</u>

3. A long novel is not necessarily a hard one to follow.　　<u>**to follow**</u>

4. Lending a good book to a friend can be very satisfying.　　<u>**none**</u>

5. If you want nothing except to escape, read a fantasy adventure.　　<u>**to escape**</u>

6. If you want to learn, read a more serious book.　　<u>**to learn**</u>

7. Whether a book is light or serious, read to understand.　　<u>**to understand**</u>

8. For some books a quick way to read is to skim.　　<u>**to read, to skim**</u>

9. If you are willing to concentrate, a difficult book is worthwhile.　　<u>**to concentrate**</u>

10. Some books are good enough to reread.　　<u>**to reread**</u>

A **participle** is a verb form used as an adjective. You can use the present participle and the past participle forms as verbals.

Verb	Present participle	Past participle
climb	climbing	climbed
burst	bursting	burst
pay	paying	paid
think	thinking	thought
spring	springing	sprung
break	breaking	broken
know	knowing	known
take	taking	taken

Since participles act as adjectives, they modify nouns or pronouns.

The **blinding** storm kept the climbers indoors for several more days.

The **trained** guide went out into the snow.

His **forgotten** pick lay on the table.

A participle can come either before or after the noun or pronoun that it modifies.

Chilled and **exhausted,** most of the climbers returned home after an hour.

Those **remaining** left shortly afterward.

GUIDED PRACTICE

What is the participle in each sentence? Which word does it modify?

Example: Trained mountain climbers always plan carefully.
trained   climbers

1. A challenging mountain offers excitement to a climber.
2. Experienced climbers look for new mountains to climb.
3. Spiked boots are one necessary piece of equipment.
4. Climbers also use ropes, axes, and specialized tools.
5. Good climbers, tiring, will rest where they can.
6. Those resting will check their equipment and their route.

REMINDER

- A **verbal** is a word that is formed from a verb. Verbals are used as nouns, adjectives, or adverbs.
- A **participle** is a verbal used as an adjective.

Blinding lights flood the **crowded** theater.

Those **watching** cannot guess the play's **surprising** outcome.

INDEPENDENT PRACTICE

Write the participles that modify the underlined words in these sentences.

Example: Every year the eighth grade sees an exciting <u>play</u> on Broadway.
exciting

1. Experienced and prepared, the <u>actors</u> always give a superb performance.
   Experienced, prepared

2. <u>Those</u> seated enjoy an unobstructed <u>view</u> of the stage.
   seated, unobstructed

3. Then the students take a guided <u>tour</u> of Manhattan.
   guided

4. Towering <u>buildings</u> and flashing <u>lights</u> are everywhere.
   Towering, flashing

5. They listen to the astounding <u>history</u> of the Brooklyn Bridge.
   astounding

6. The <u>Chrysler Building</u>, striking and shining, delights them.
   striking, shining

7. Later the class enjoys an inspiring <u>concert</u> at Carnegie Hall.
   inspiring

8. Then the <u>students</u>, exhausted and worn, return home by train.
   exhausted, worn

You know that a phrase is a group of words that is used as a single word in a sentence. A phrase does not have a subject or a predicate.

in the United States

Unlike a phrase, a **clause** is a group of words that does have a subject and a predicate.

subj. pred.
Alaska is the largest state

Because a sentence always contains a subject and a predicate, every sentence contains at least one clause. Not every sentence contains a phrase, however.

A clause that can stand by itself as a sentence is called a **main clause,** or an **independent clause.**

Alaska became a state in 1959

A clause that cannot stand by itself as a sentence is a **dependent clause,** or a **subordinate clause.**

when Alaska became a state

A **subordinating conjunction** is a word used to introduce a subordinate clause. You can turn an independent clause into a subordinate clause by adding a subordinating conjunction.

INDEPENDENT
we visited Alaska's coast
Eskimos hunt and fish

SUBORDINATE
when we visited Alaska's coast
where Eskimos hunt and fish

Common Subordinating Conjunctions			
after	because	so that	when
although	before	than	whenever
as	even though	that	where
as if	if	though	wherever
as soon as	in order that	unless	while
as though	since	until	

Do not confuse clauses that begin with *after, before, since,* or *until* with phrases that begin with these words. Remember that a clause has a subject and a verb.

PHRASE: People flocked to Alaska **after discoveries of gold**
CLAUSE: People flocked to Alaska **after gold was discovered**

Is each group of words a phrase or a clause?

Example: the United States purchased Alaska   *clause*

1.   from the Russian government   phrase
2.   for only about two cents an acre   phrase
3.   many Americans ridiculed the purchase of this cold place   clause
4.   although the state has valuable resources   clause

REMINDER

- A **phrase** does not contain a subject and a predicate.
- A **clause** contains both a subject and a predicate.
- An **independent clause** can stand by itself as a sentence.
- A **subordinate clause** cannot stand by itself as a sentence.

Phrase	**Clause**
	subject predicate
since colonial days	**since** the colonists arrived
Independent Clause	**Subordinate Clause**
Hudson explored the coast	**when** Hudson explored the coast

INDEPENDENT PRACTICE

Label each underlined clause *independent* or *subordinate*.

1.   Because Cornelius May sailed the Delaware River, Cape May is named for him.   subordinate

2.   After some exploration, the Dutch created a settlement in New Jersey.   independent

3.   As soon as the British gained control of New Amsterdam, they also gained control of New Jersey.   subordinate

4.   During the early years of British control, New Jersey consisted of two colonies.   independent

Compound and Complex Sentences

Now that you have learned about the two types of clauses — independent and subordinate — you can use them to form different kinds of sentences.

1. A **simple sentence** is an independent clause that stands by itself.

    independent
    Sponges are primitive animals.

2. A **compound sentence** contains two or more combined independent clauses.

    independent   independent
    Water enters a sponge, and **the sponge grows larger.**

3. A **complex sentence** contains one or more subordinate clauses combined with an independent clause.

    independent   subordinate
    A sponge absorbs water as if it contained many mouths.

    independent   subordinate   subordinate
    A sponge is odd because it grows back after it is torn.

Remember the difference between coordinating conjunctions and subordinating conjunctions. Coordinating conjunctions connect independent clauses to form compound sentences. Subordinating conjunctions connect subordinate clauses with independent clauses to form complex sentences.

COORDINATING CONJUNCTION: I wet the sponge, **and** it expanded.
SUBORDINATING CONJUNCTION: I wet the sponge **until** it expanded.

GUIDED PRACTICE

Is each sentence simple, compound, or complex?

Example: Because it has no muscles, nerves, or organs, a sponge is considered a primitive animal.   *complex*

1. A sponge feeds as it filters water.   **complex**
2. Water carries food and bacteria into the sponge.   **simple**
3. Sponges live on reefs where many animals make their homes.   **complex**
4. The sea star is one of the sponge's few enemies.   **simple**
5. The sizes and colors of sponges vary, but their basic processes are the same.   **compound**
6. All sponges pump water through their canals, and even a small sponge can pump thirty gallons a day.   **compound**

REMINDER

- A **simple sentence** is an independent clause that stands by itself.
- A **compound sentence** contains two or more independent clauses.
- A **complex sentence** contains at least one subordinate clause and an independent clause.

Simple Sentence:	independent Sir Edmund Hillary climbed Mt. Everest.
Compound Sentence:	independent independent He climbed it first , and others followed .
Complex Sentence:	subordinate independent After he climbed it , others followed .

INDEPENDENT PRACTICE

Label each sentence *simple*, *compound*, or *complex*.

Example: Many tried to reach the top, but most failed.   **compound**

1. Mt. Everest is the tallest mountain in the world.   simple

2. It is tall, but Sir Edmund Hillary conquered it.   compound

3. Because it is so tall, it is difficult to climb.   complex

4. It is dangerous on Mt. Everest, where avalanches occur.   complex

5. Strong winds blow, and avalanches occur often.   compound

6. Avalanches occur often on Mt. Everest.   simple

7. The mountain is very steep, and the air at the peak is thin.   compound

8. The mountain is very steep and dangerous.   simple

9. Because the mountain is very steep, climbing it is dangerous if you are unprepared.   complex

10. Hillary was from New Zealand.   simple

11. Although Hillary was from New Zealand, the expedition was British.   complex

12. He was from New Zealand, but the expedition was British.   compound

Abbreviations

Abbreviations are shortened forms of words. Most abbreviations begin with a capital letter and end with a period.

Titles		
Mr. Juan Alba *(Mister)*	John Helt, Sr. *(Senior)*
Mrs. Ida Wong *(Mistress)*	John Helt, Jr. *(Junior)*
Ms. Leslie Clark	Dr. Jill Todd *(Doctor)*

NOTE: Miss is not an abbreviation and does not end with a period.

Words used in addresses		
St. *(Street)*	Rte. *(Route)*
Rd. *(Road)*	Apt. *(Apartment)*
Ave. *(Avenue)*	Mt. *(Mount or Mountain)*
Dr. *(Drive)*	Expy. *(Expressway)*
Blvd. *(Boulevard)*	Pkwy. *(Parkway)*

Words used in business		
Co. *(Company)*	Corp. *(Corporation)*
Ltd. *(Limited)*	Inc. *(Incorporated)*

Other abbreviations

Some abbreviations are written in all capital letters, with a letter standing for each important word.

P.D. *(Police Department)*	P.O. *(Post Office)*
R.N. *(Registered Nurse)*	M.A. *(Master of Arts)*

Some abbreviations have neither capital letters nor periods.

mph *(miles per hour)*   hp *(horsepower)*   ft *(feet)*

Some abbreviations begin with a small letter and end with a period.

gal. *(gallon)*   p. *(page)*   min. *(minute)*

Abbreviations of government agencies or national organizations do not usually have periods.

IRS *(Internal Revenue Service)*
NBA *(National Basketball Association)*

Days of the week		
Mon. *(Monday)*	Fri. *(Friday)*
Tues. *(Tuesday)*	Sat. *(Saturday)*
Wed. *(Wednesday)*	Sun. *(Sunday)*
Thurs. *(Thursday)*	

CAPITALIZATION, PUNCTUATION, USAGE

Abbreviations continued

Months of the Year	Jan. *(January)*	Sept. *(September)*
	Feb. *(February)*	Oct. *(October)*
	Mar. *(March)*	Nov. *(November)*
	Apr. *(April)*	Dec. *(December)*
	Aug. *(August)*	
	May, June, and *July* are not abbreviated.	

States

The United States Postal Service uses two capital letters and no period in each of its state abbreviations.

AL *(Alabama)*	MT *(Montana)*
AK *(Alaska)*	NE *(Nebraska)*
AZ *(Arizona)*	NV *(Nevada)*
AR *(Arkansas)*	NH *(New Hampshire)*
CA *(California)*	NJ *(New Jersey)*
CO *(Colorado)*	NM *(New Mexico)*
CT *(Connecticut)*	NY *(New York)*
DE *(Delaware)*	NC *(North Carolina)*
FL *(Florida)*	ND *(North Dakota)*
GA *(Georgia)*	OH *(Ohio)*
HI *(Hawaii)*	OK *(Oklahoma)*
ID *(Idaho)*	OR *(Oregon)*
IL *(Illinois)*	PA *(Pennsylvania)*
IN *(Indiana)*	RI *(Rhode Island)*
IA *(Iowa)*	SC *(South Carolina)*
KS *(Kansas)*	SD *(South Dakota)*
KY *(Kentucky)*	TN *(Tennessee)*
LA *(Louisiana)*	TX *(Texas)*
ME *(Maine)*	UT *(Utah)*
MD *(Maryland)*	VT *(Vermont)*
MA *(Massachusetts)*	VA *(Virginia)*
MI *(Michigan)*	WA *(Washington)*
MN *(Minnesota)*	WV *(West Virginia)*
MS *(Mississippi)*	WI *(Wisconsin)*
MO *(Missouri)*	WY *(Wyoming)*

Bibliography

The basic organization of a bibliography is alphabetical, although entries can be grouped by the type of reference materials used: books, encyclopedias, magazines. If the author's name is not given, list the title first and alphabetize it by the first important word of the title.

Bibliography continued

Books   List the author's name (last name first), the book title (underlined), the city where the publisher is located, the publisher's name, and the year of publication. Note the punctuation.

Smith, Whitney. The Flag Book of the United States. New York: William Morrow, 1970.

Encyclopedia article   List the author's name (last name first) and then the title of the article (in quotation marks). Next, give the title of the encyclopedia (underlined), and the year of publication of the edition that you are using. Note the punctuation.

Dertouzos, Michael. "Personal Computer." The World Book Encyclopedia. 1986 ed.

If the author of the article is not given, begin your listing with the title of the article.

"Charles River." Collier's Encyclopedia. 1980 ed.

Magazine or newspaper article   List the author's name (last name first), the title of the article (in quotation marks), the name of the magazine or newspaper (underlined), the date of publication, the section in which the article appears (for newspaper articles only), and the page numbers of the article.

MAGAZINE: Horst, John. "Making a Sundial." Country Journal, March 1980, pp. 97–99.

NEWSPAPER: "Train Snarls Downtown Traffic." Somerville News, Jan. 6, 1986, Sec. A, p. 5.

Here is another way that you can write these entries:

MAGAZINE: Horst, John. "Making a Sundial." Country Journal March 1980: 97–99.

NEWSPAPER: "Train Snarls Downtown Traffic." Somerville News 6 Jan. 1986, sec. A:5.

Titles

Underlining   Titles of books, magazines, newspapers, plays, movies, television series, works of art, musical compositions, planes, trains, ships, and spacecraft are underlined.

The Meantime *(book)*	Nova *(TV series)*
Seventeen *(magazine)*	Waterlilies *(painting)*
Daily News *(newspaper)*	Skylab *(spacecraft)*

CAPITALIZATION, PUNCTUATION, USAGE

Quotation marks | Titles of short stories, articles, songs, poems, and book chapters are enclosed in quotation marks.

"The Fox" *(short story)*   "If" *(poem)*
"Sand Skiing" *(article)*   "Celtic Art" *(chapter)*
"America" *(song)*

Quotations

Quotation marks with commas and periods | Quotation marks are used to set a speaker's exact words apart from the rest of a sentence. Commas separate the quotation. The first word begins with a capital letter.

"Please put away your books," said Mr. Emory.

Linda asked, "When is the report due?"

Sometimes a quotation is divided into two parts. Enclose each part in quotation marks. If the second part of the divided quotation continues the original sentence, begin it with a small letter. If it starts a new sentence, begin it with a capital letter.

"Where," asked the stranger, "is the post office?"

"I must mail a letter," he added. "It is urgent."

Always place a period inside closing quotation marks. Place a question mark or an exclamation point outside closing quotation marks unless the quotation itself is a question or an exclamation.

Did the stranger really say, "This is top secret"?

Frank exclaimed, "Look at the beautiful baby!"

Dialogue | In dialogues, begin a new paragraph whenever the speaker changes.

"Where is Bangladesh?" asked our history teacher, Ms. Collins.

"I think that it is in India," said Ellen.

"No," said Greg. "It used to be part of Pakistan, but now it is an independent nation."

Indirect quotations | An indirect quotation tells what a person has said without using that person's exact words. Do not use quotation marks to set off indirect quotations.

Wendy mentioned that she had to go to the library.

CAPITALIZATION, PUNCTUATION, USAGE

Rules for capitalization	**Capitalize the first word of every sentence.** What an unusual color the roses are!
	Capitalize the pronoun _I_. What should I do next?
	Capitalize every important word in the names of particular people, places, or things.

Emily G. Hesse   Lincoln Memorial
District of Columbia   Bill of Rights

Capitalize titles or their abbreviations when used with a person's name.

Governor Bradford   Senator Smith   Dr. Lin

Capitalize proper adjectives.
We ate at a Hungarian restaurant.   She is French.

Capitalize the names of months and days.
My birthday is on the last Monday in March.

Capitalize the names of organizations, businesses, institutions, and agencies.
National Hockey League   The Status Company

Capitalize the names of periods, holidays, and other special events.
Bronze Age   Industrial Revolution   Labor Day

Capitalize the first and last words and all important words in the titles of books, newspapers, magazines, stories, songs, poems, reports, and outlines. (Articles, short conjunctions, and short prepositions are not capitalized unless they are the first or last word.)

Julie of the Wolves   "Over the Rainbow"
The New York Times   "The Road Not Taken"
Farm Journal   "Canadian National Parks"
"Growing Up"   "The Exports of Italy"

Capitalize the first word of each main topic and subtopic in an outline.

I.   Types of libraries
   A.   Large public library
   B.   Bookmobile

CAPITALIZATION, PUNCTUATION, USAGE

Rules for capitalization (continued)	**Capitalize the first word in the greeting and closing of a letter.** Dear Marcia,　　Yours truly,
	Capitalize nationalities, languages, religions, and religious terms. Chinese　　Spanish　　American　　Buddhism
	Capitalize words showing family relationships only when they are used before a name or when they take the place of a name. Today Uncle Jerry is coming. My uncle and I are good friends.
	Capitalize cities, counties, states, countries, continents, and regions of the United States. London　　Iowa　　Asia Essex County　　Canada　　the South
	Capitalize streets, highways, buildings, bridges, and monuments. Fifth Avenue　　London Bridge Interstate 90　　Statue of Liberty Empire State Building
	Capitalize planets, bodies of water, and geographic features. Saturn　　Andes Mountains Indian Ocean　　Sahara Desert
	Capitalize the names of documents. Declaration of Independence Atomic Energy Act

Punctuation

End marks	**There are three end marks. A *period (.)* ends a declarative or imperative sentence. A *question mark (?)* follows an interrogative sentence. An *exclamation point (!)* follows an exclamatory sentence.** The scissors are on my desk. *(declarative)* Look up the spelling of that word. *(imperative)* How is the word spelled? *(interrogative)* This is your best poem so far! *(exclamatory)*

Interjections	An *interjection* is a word or group of words that expresses feeling. It is followed by a comma or an exclamation point. My goodness, this tastes terrible. Hurray! The field goal counts.
Apostrophe	**To form the possessive of a singular noun, add an apostrophe and *s*.** baby's grandmother's sister-in-law's family's
	For a plural noun that ends in *s*, add an apostrophe only. sisters' families' Smiths' hound dogs'
	For a plural noun that does not end in *s*, add an apostrophe and *s*. women's alumni's mice's sisters-in-law's
	Use an apostrophe in contractions in place of dropped letters. isn't *(is not)* they've *(they have)* can't *(cannot)* we're *(we are)* won't *(will not)* it's *(it is)* I'm *(I am)* they'll *(they will)*
Colon	**Use a colon in the greeting of a business letter.** Dear Mrs. Trimby: Dear Realty Homes:
	Use a colon to introduce a list. I like the following foods: fish, peas, and pears.
	Use a colon when writing the time of day. They came back from lunch at 1:04 P.M.
Comma	**Use commas to separate words in a series.** Clyde asked if we had any apples, peaches, or grapes.
	Use a comma to separate the simple sentences in a compound sentence. Some students were at lunch, but we were studying.
	Use commas to set off an appositive from the rest of the sentence when the appositive is not necessary to the meaning of the sentence. The poet Emily Dickinson lived a quiet life. *(The appositive is necessary to the meaning.)* Massachusetts, the Bay State, has lovely beaches. *(The appositive is not necessary to the meaning.)*

CAPITALIZATION, PUNCTUATION, USAGE

Comma (continued)	**Use commas after introductory words such as *yes, no,* and *well.***	
	Well, it's just too cold out. No, it isn't six yet.	
	Use commas to set off interrupters such as *however, for example, in my opinion,* and *as a matter of fact.*	
	London, however, never bored him.	
	Use a comma to separate a noun in direct address from the rest of the sentence.	
	Jean, help me fix this tire. How was your trip, Jo?	
	Use a comma to separate the month and day from the year.	
	Use a comma to separate the year from the rest of the sentence.	
	June 17, 1951, is Maureen's birthday.	
	Use a comma between the names of a city and a state or a city and a country.	
	Chicago, Illinois Caracas, Venezuela	
	Use a comma between a street and a city when they appear in a sentence but not between the state and the ZIP code.	
	I live at 29 Bear Brook Lane, Provo, Utah 84604.	
	Use a comma after the greeting in a friendly letter and after the closing in all letters.	
	Dear Deena, Sincerely yours,	
	Use a comma following an introductory prepositional phrase.	
	Inside the right-hand cabinet, you will find a ruler.	
Semicolon	**A semicolon can be used to separate the parts of a compound sentence.**	
	It was very late; we decided to go to bed.	
Hyphens, dashes, and parentheses	**Use a hyphen to join the parts of compound numbers, to join two or more words that work together as one adjective before a noun, or to divide a word at the end of a line.**	
	sixty-one well-developed paragraph	
	Raphael is known as one of Italy's many magnif-icent painters.	

Punctuation continued

Hyphens, dashes, and parentheses (continued)	**Use dashes to show a break of thought in a sentence.** The paintings — curiously enough — are done in oil.	
	Use parentheses to enclose an explanation that is not of major importance to a sentence. Read Chapter 2 (page 67) for more information.	

Problem Words

Words	Rules	Examples
a, an, the	The indefinite articles *a* and *an* refer to any one of a group of things. The definite article *the* refers to a particular thing or several particular things.	Eat a piece of fruit. The pear was delicious.
a, an	Use *a* and *an* before singular nouns. Use *a* before a word that begins with a consonant sound. Use *an* before a word that begins with a vowel sound.	a banana an hour
the	Use *the* with other singular and plural nouns.	the apple the apples
bad	*Bad* is an adjective. It can be used after linking verbs like *look* and *feel*.	This was a bad day. I feel bad.
badly	*Badly* is an adverb.	I play badly.
beside	*Beside* means "next to."	He is working beside me.
besides	*Besides* means "in addition to."	Who, besides Dan, is working?

CAPITALIZATION, PUNCTUATION, USAGE

Problem Words continued

Words	Rules	Examples
between	*Between* refers to two people, places, or things.	I stood between John and Ann.
among	*Among* refers to three or more people, places, or things.	I stood among the crowd.
bring	*Bring* means "to carry or lead toward the speaker."	Please bring me the book.
take	*Take* means "to carry or lead away from the speaker."	I will take the book to him.
fewer	Use *fewer* or *fewest* with nouns that can be counted.	Fewer boys are here today.
less	Use *less* or *least* with nouns that cannot be counted.	I have the least money.
good	*Good* is an adjective.	The weather looks good.
well	*Well* is usually an adverb. It is used as an adjective only when it refers to health.	She swims well. Do you feel well?
its	*Its* is a possessive pronoun.	The dog wagged its tail.
it's	*It's* is a contraction of *it is.*	It's cold today.
lend	The verb *lend* means "to give something temporarily."	Please lend me some money.
loan	The noun *loan* means "the act of lending" or "the thing lent."	David gave me a loan.
let	*Let* means "to permit or allow."	Please let me go swimming.
leave	*Leave* means "to go away from" or "to allow to remain."	I will leave soon. Leave it on my desk.

Words	Rules	Examples
lie	*Lie* means "to rest or remain in one place."	The dog <u>lies</u> on the rug.
lay	*Lay* means "to put something down."	Please <u>lay</u> the books here.
raise	*Raise* means "to lift," "to move up," "to increase," or "to grow."	Please <u>raise</u> the window. The store <u>raised</u> prices. Maggie <u>raises</u> tomatoes.
rise	*Rise* means "to get up or go up."	This elevator <u>rises</u> slowly.
set	*Set* means "to place or put."	<u>Set</u> the vase on the table.
sit	*Sit* means "to take a seat; to be seated."	Please <u>sit</u> in this chair.
their	*Their* is a possessive pronoun.	<u>Their</u> coats are on the bed.
there	*There* is an adverb. It may also begin a sentence.	Is Carlos <u>there</u>? <u>There</u> is my book.
they're	*They're* is a contraction of *they are.*	<u>They're</u> going to the store.
theirs	*Theirs* is a possessive pronoun.	This dog is <u>theirs</u>.
there's	*There's* is a contraction of *there is.*	<u>There's</u> his tag.
this, these	Use *this* and *these* for things that are close by.	<u>This</u> is my room, and <u>these</u> are my books.
that, those	Use *that* and *those* for things that are far away.	<u>That</u> is Jill over there. <u>Those</u> are mountains.
whose	*Whose* is a possessive pronoun.	<u>Whose</u> tickets are these?
who's	*Who's* is a contraction for *who is.*	<u>Who's</u> that woman?
your	*Your* is a possessive pronoun.	Are these <u>your</u> glasses?
you're	*You're* is a contraction for *you are.*	<u>You're</u> late again!

Comparing	**To compare two things, add *-er* to adjectives and adverbs or use the word *more*.** This tree is taller than the other one. It grew more quickly.
	To compare three or more things, add *-est* or use the word *most*. This tree is the tallest of the three. It grew most quickly.
	Use *more* or *most* when the adjective or adverb is a long word. agreeable – more agreeable – most agreeable
	When you compare things, actions, or qualities that are *less* rather than *more*, use *less* for the comparative and *least* for the superlative. quickly – less quickly – least quickly
Double comparisons	**Avoid double comparisons.** She is a better (*not* more better) skier than he. She skis faster (*not* more faster) than her brother.
Irregular adjectives and adverbs	**Some adjectives and adverbs have irregular forms. Since they do not follow the normal rules, these forms must be memorized.**

Positive	*Comparative*	*Superlative*
good/well	better	best
bad/badly	worse	worst
little	less	least
much/many	more	most
far	farther	farthest

Adjective and adverb phrases	**Place an adjective phrase right after the word that it modifies.** The museum in Philadelphia has a special exhibit.
	Place an adverb phrase near the word that it modifies or at the beginning of a sentence. For two months, it will display Diego Rivera's art.
real, really sure, surely	***Real*** and ***sure*** are adjectives. ***Really*** and ***surely*** are adverbs. This ring is made of real gold. He is a really good skater. Pat was sure of her answer. He surely is an excellent cook.

A negative word or contraction says "no" or "not." *Barely*, *hardly*, and *scarcely* are considered negative words. Do not use two negatives to express one negative idea. One way to correct a double negative is to substitute a positive word for a negative one.

INCORRECT:	I didn't hardly have enough time.
CORRECT:	I hardly had enough time.
INCORRECT:	Won't nobody come with me?
CORRECT:	Won't anybody come with me?

Pronoun Usage

Agreement

A pronoun must agree with the noun to which it refers. This noun is called its antecedent.

Kee bought a newspaper, but May read it first.

Jeff and Kim came to lunch. They enjoyed the meal.

When it was finished, the sculpture was beautiful.

Demonstrative pronouns must agree in number with the nouns to which they refer.
This is Copley Square.
These are the famous cherry trees.
Is that the Golden Gate Bridge?
Those are fine examples of Greek columns.

Indefinite pronouns

An *indefinite pronoun* does not refer to a specific person or thing. When you use an indefinite pronoun as a subject, the verb must agree with it.

SINGULAR:	Everyone is invited. Neither is here.
PLURAL:	Several were invited. Many are here.

Pronouns must agree with indefinite pronouns used as antecedents.
Each has its own name. Others lost their books.
Everyone found her way into the cafeteria.

Subject and object pronouns

Use a *subject pronoun* as the subject of a sentence or as a predicate pronoun (after a linking verb).
He arrived late. The only girl in line is she.

C A P I T A L I Z A T I O N , P U N C T U A T I O N , U S A G E

Subject and object pronouns (continued)	**Use an *object pronoun* as a direct object of the verb, as an indirect object, or as an object of the preposition.** Clyde collected old coins and sold <u>them</u>. *(direct object)* She gave <u>him</u> the flower. *(indirect object)* Share these bananas with <u>her</u>. *(object of preposition)*
Compound subjects or objects	**To choose the correct pronoun in a compound subject or compound object, say the sentence with the pronoun alone.** Tom and <u>I</u> looked for Bob. *(I looked for Bob.)* We found Mary, Alice, and <u>him</u>. *(We found him.)*
Possessive pronouns	**Most possessive pronouns have two forms. One is used before nouns. The other is used alone.** <u>My</u> friend Otoki and I looked at kimonos. She showed me <u>hers</u>.
Reflexive and intensive pronouns	**Do not use reflexive or intensive pronouns in place of personal pronouns.** INCORRECT: Jennifer and <u>myself</u> will be late. CORRECT: Jennifer and <u>I</u> will be late. INCORRECT: I'm going with Dan and <u>yourself</u>. CORRECT: I'm going with Dan and <u>you</u>.
	Do not use *hisself* or *theirselves.* Adam will do that <u>himself</u> (*not* hisself). They gave <u>themselves</u> (*not* theirselves) a head start.
I, me	***I* is used as a subject. *Me* is used as an object. (See *Subject and object pronouns*.)** Jan and <u>I</u> are going to the show. She is taking <u>me</u>.
	When using *I* or *me* with other nouns or pronouns, name yourself last. Beth and <u>I</u> will leave. Please help <u>him and me</u>.
we, us	**To use the pronoun *we* or *us* correctly with a noun in a sentence, first look at the noun. If the noun is the subject of the sentence or if it follows a linking verb, use the pronoun *we* with it. If it is the object, use *us.*** <u>We</u> (*not* Us) students are proud. The winners are <u>we</u> (*not* us) girls. The award was for <u>us</u> (*not* we) students.

Tenses	**When a sentence describes actions that took place at two different times, use the past perfect for the earlier action and the past tense for the later action.** Bob <u>had trained</u> hard, but he <u>lost</u> the match anyway.
	When a sentence describes two actions in the future, use the future perfect for the earlier action and the present for the later action. She <u>will have stopped</u> before the bell <u>rings</u>.
	Avoid unnecessary shifts from one tense to another. A train <u>appeared</u>, but no one <u>was</u> (*not* is) on board.
Agreement: compound subjects	**A compound subject with *and* takes a plural verb.** <u>Jason</u>, <u>Kelly</u>, and <u>Wanda</u> <u>have</u> new dictionaries.
	A compound subject with *or* or *nor* takes a verb that agrees with the nearer subject. She or her <u>cousins</u> <u>are</u> ready to help. Her <u>cousins</u> or <u>Paula</u> <u>is</u> ready to help.
Agreement: inverted order, interrupted order	**Subject and verb must agree, no matter where the subject is. First, find the subject; then make the verb agree with it.** In the pond <u>were</u> several <u>frogs</u>. The <u>show</u> of photographs <u>is</u> now open.
Irregular verbs	**Irregular verbs, unlike regular verbs, do not add *-ed* or *-d* to form the past participle. The principal parts of these verbs must be memorized. Always use a form of the verb *have* with the past participle.**

Verb	Past	Past Participle
be	was	been
bite	bit	bitten
blow	blew	blown
break	broke	broken
buy	bought	bought
catch	caught	caught

Irregular verbs (continued)	Verb	Past	Past Participle
	choose	chose	chosen
	come	came	come
	do	did	done
	draw	drew	drawn
	drink	drank	drunk
	drive	drove	driven
	eat	ate	eaten
	fall	fell	fallen
	feel	felt	felt
	fight	fought	fought
	fly	flew	flown
	freeze	froze	frozen
	get	got	gotten
	give	gave	given
	go	went	gone
	grow	grew	grown
	have	had	had
	hide	hid	hidden
	know	knew	known
	lose	lost	lost
	make	made	made
	put	put	put
	ride	rode	ridden
	ring	rang	rung
	run	ran	run
	say	said	said
	see	saw	seen
	shake	shook	shaken
	shrink	shrank	shrunk
	shut	shut	shut
	sing	sang	sung
	sleep	slept	slept
	speak	spoke	spoken
	stand	stood	stood
	steal	stole	stolen
	swim	swam	swum
	tear	tore	torn
	tell	told	told
	think	thought	thought
	throw	threw	thrown
	wear	wore	worn
	write	wrote	written

Modeling the Lessons

Page 155
Conjunctions   Have students first name foods they like and then foods they dislike. Appoint two volunteers to write the students' suggestions on the board.

Write on the board the common coordinating (*and, but, or*) and correlative (*both . . . and, either . . . or, neither . . . nor, whether . . . or*) conjunctions, without labeling them. Ask students to join items in the food lists with conjunctions to form complete sentences. (For example: We like carrots, but we don't like fish. Both tomatoes and oranges are fruit.) You may wish to have students draw conclusions about the relationships shown in the sentences.

Page 157
Combining Sentences: Complex Sentences   Ask students to answer the following question with simple sentences: If you found a treasure chest that contained something you have always wanted, what would that something be and what would you do with it? Write some of the students' answers on the board. Have students use these sentences to create complex sentences. Then have students change the conjunctions in two of the complex sentences and discuss how the meanings of the sentences have been changed.

Emphasize that a compound sentence simply states that two events occurred. A complex sentence makes clear how the events are related.

Page 159
Kinds of Nouns   Bring a variety of objects to class. (For example: zipper, camera, stapler) Have students identify each object and write its name in a column on the board. Tell students they are now time travelers visiting a tribe of cave people. Have students describe some of the emotions the cave dwellers might feel seeing the objects brought by the students. Look for such words as *puzzlement, fear,* and *doubt.* Write these on the board in a second column. Ask what the words in each column have in common. How are the two columns different? (Words in column 1 name concrete things; words in column 2 name feelings.)

Page 161
Combining Sentences: Appositives
Write these two sentences on the board:

The animal blocked the road.
The animal was a black bear.

Ask students how they could combine the sentences to make them less choppy. (The animal, a black bear, blocked the road.) Write the new sentence on the board. Ask students to give an example of two sentences that could be combined in the same way. Then have students combine their example sentences, using an appositive. Explain that when an appositive comes at the end of the sentence, only one comma is used.

Page 163
Verb Phrases   Remind students that a simple predicate may consist of more than one word. Ask students to describe the weather of the preceding week, and write some of the sentences on the board. Ask if they know the forecast for the next few days, and write some of these sentences as well. Have students identify the simple predicate in each sentence. Which predicates have more than one word? Which word is the most important? (that which expresses action or being)

Page 165
Forms of *be, have,* and *do*   Have students review the forms of the simple tenses. Ask them if tenses of all verbs can be formed in the same way. Help students to realize they cannot, and have them think of some exceptions. Write the exceptions on the board. Students should conclude from the examples they have given that some verb forms are irregular and must be memorized because they do not follow the general rules for forming verb tenses.

Page 167
Perfect Tenses   Have students review and conjugate the simple tenses of the verb *have: have, had,* and *will have.* Ask students how the verb *have* functions in the following sentence: *By tomorrow I will have completed the project.* (as a helping verb) Ask students if the verb in this sentence fits any of the tenses they have studied thus far. (no) Lead them to conclude that other verb tenses are needed

to express past and future actions in different ways.

Page 169
Direct and Indirect Objects   Ask students to name insects they fear or do not like. (For example: scorpions, cockroaches) Have them give their reasons. (They sting us. They spread disease.) Use student responses to show the relationship between transitive verbs and direct objects. Then write two sentences on the board. (For example: I asked you a question. You gave me an answer.) Have volunteers identify the verbs of each sentence and suggest what the noun or pronoun after each verb does. (It tells who or what is affected by the action of the verb.)

Page 171
Predicate Nouns and Predicate Adjectives   Talk about your favorite author and explain your reasons for liking his or her books. Ask students for the names of their favorite authors and favorite books and have them explain why they like them. Record some of their responses on the board. (For example: Robert Newton Peck is my favorite author.) Ask students to identify the complete predicate and kind of verb in each sentence. Lead students to observe that linking verbs have different complements than action verbs have.

Page 173
Active and Passive Voices   Write on the board a sentence that contains a verb in the active voice. (For example: The cheetah chased the gazelle.) Ask students to identify the verb. Is it an action verb or a linking verb? (action verb) Then ask them to identify the direct object and the subject, or doer, of the action.

Challenge students to reword the sentence so that the subject is the receiver of the action. (The gazelle was chased by the cheetah.)

Page 175
Subject-Verb Agreement   Find out which students play musical instruments or sing. Make one list of student names and a second list of instruments or vocal qualities, such as the following:

Jody	piano
Elaine	alto

After the lists are complete, have students suggest sentences that include

singular, plural, and compound subjects. Ask students how they knew which form of the verb to use in each of the sentences. (by the number of the subject)

Page 177
Being Verbs and Linking Verbs   Ask students to give sentences that describe a place they've visited. Write on the board several sentences that use linking verbs. (For example: Memphis is a southern city. It seems very large.) Have students identify the verb in each sentence (is, seems), and discuss with them how the linking verb connects the subject to words that tell more about it. Have students identify which sentences have a noun in the predicate that renames the subject. (Memphis is a southern city.) Then have them identify sentences that have an adjective in the predicate that describes the subject. (It seems very large.)

Page 179
Pronouns and Antecedents   Write a paragraph on the board in which no pronouns are used. For example:

> Leo lost Leo's hat. Leo's hat was old. Leo's sister bought Leo a new hat on sale. Leo promised Leo's sister Leo would never lose Leo's hat again.

Ask students to comment on the paragraph. (For example: How does it sound? What words would you replace?) Have volunteers suggest alternatives to the awkward-sounding phrases. Students should know that there are words that can be substituted for nouns.

Page 181
Pronouns in Compound Subjects and Objects   Ask volunteers to review for the class compound subjects and direct and indirect objects. Then question students about dances they have learned or dancing classes they have taken. Write some of their statements on the board, using complete sentences.

> Ken and Ada know how to square-dance. They taught Marie and Howard some dance steps.

Have students combine sentences using pronouns in compound subjects or compound objects.

Page 183
Interrogative Pronouns   Write these sentences on the board:

> He is reading a book.
> Ivy gave the book to him.
> The book used to be hers.

Ask volunteers to identify and underline the pronouns. Then ask students to suppose that the sentences are answers to questions and that the underlined words give the information that was asked for. What question does *He is reading a book* answer? (*Who* is reading a book?) Ask what questions the other statements answer, and write them on the board as students give them. (To *whom* did Ivy give the book? *Whose* book did that used to be?) Underline *who, whom,* and *whose.* Tell students that these words are examples of another kind of pronoun.

Page 185
Demonstrative Pronouns   Show different pictures of groups of various objects, some of which are closer and others farther away. (For example: buildings, foods, crafts) Ask students to describe one of the objects. As students make up sentences, ask them to specify which of the objects is being described and to point it out. If students do not automatically use a demonstrative pronoun, ask questions such as "Is this the one?" After several repetitions, have students name the words that both you and they used to demonstrate specific objects. (For example: *this, that, these, those*)

Page 187
Indefinite Pronouns   Begin a discussion of pet peeves and have students propose some examples. (For example: someone's talking during a movie) As the discussion continues, ask questions such as "Do many of you feel this way?" and "Have all of you experienced this?" After a while, write on the board some of the indefinite pronouns that were used. Ask students if these words stand for something definite or something indefinite. (indefinite) Use a sentence from the discussion as an example, and ask students if they can identify the antecedent of the pronoun. Point out to them that an indefinite pronoun does not have a clear antecedent.

Page 189
Adjective Phrases   Write a paragraph like the following on the board.

> The children from _____ entered the kitchen. They saw a jar of _____. It was sitting in a basket of _____. The basket was made from _____.

Ask students to fill in the blanks. Can students determine what the prepositional phrases tell about the words that immediately precede them? (which one, what kind) What other part of speech modifies words in the same way? (adjectives)

Page 191
Adverb Phrases   Ask for volunteers to review what an adverb does. (It modifies verbs, adjectives, and other adverbs. It tells *how, when, where,* or *to what extent.*) Write a sentence on the board. (For example: We rode our bikes slowly.) Have students identify the adverb (slowly) and then replace it with a prepositional phrase. (For example: on a dirt road) Ask them to identify the word modified both by the adverb and by the prepositional phrase. (the verb) What conclusions can they draw? (Prepositional phrases can be used in place of adverbs.)

Page 193
Verbals: Infinitives   Write the following sentences on the board:

> I went to gym class.
> I like to exercise.

Ask students what the phrase *to gym class* is. (prepositional phrase) Ask if *to exercise* is also a prepositional phrase. (No, prepositional phrases begin with prepositions, and those prepositions take objects.) Explain that *to exercise* is an infinitive, a form of the verb *exercise.* Ask students to tell whether *to exercise* is used as a noun, an adjective, or an adverb. (a noun)

Page 195
Verbals: Participles   Remind students that other kinds of words can also be used as adjectives. Ask for some examples. (demonstrative pronouns, possessive pronouns, and nouns) Then ask volunteers to name five verbs. Challenge students to use these verbs as adjectives in sentences. For each sentence, have students tell

whether they have used the present participle or the past participle form of the verb.

Page 197
Clauses   Write a phrase, a subordinate clause, and an independent clause on the board. For example:

1. to the west
2. because they wanted gold
3. many people traveled

Ask students to identify the groups of words in the first line. Ask them to state the difference between the first and second lines and then between the second and third lines. Have students suggest reasons why the second line is not a complete sentence. (For example: It begins with the word *because;* it does not express a complete thought.)

Explain that *subordinate* means "lower in order." A subordinate clause needs an independent clause to complete its meaning. Stress that a subordinate clause is never used alone. Without an independent clause, a subordinate clause is only a sentence fragment because it does not express a complete thought.

Page 199
Compound and Complex Sentences   Ask students to review the differences between a simple sentence and a compound sentence. Write several simple sentences on the board, such as:

Ryan cooked the dinner.
Ellie washed the dishes.
Everyone enjoyed the meal.

After the class identifies them as simple sentences, have students suggest coordinating or subordinating conjunctions, and then have the class work together to add an independent or a subordinate clause to each sentence.